The BRRRR Method

By

David Dodge and Mike Slane

CONTENTS

CHAPTER 1

Meet the Discount Property Investors

Discount Property Investors (DPI) is the new hybrid of real estate investing companies. Started by three partners, David A. Dodge, Mike Slane and Bill Maret in 2016, DPI quickly grew to one of largest real estate investing firms in the Midwest.

Each partner having built a successful real estate investing company on their own, collectively realized the power of creating a partnering co-op. We could combine our unique skills and specialties into an investing powerhouse.

DPI was founded on the concept of growth through partnership. Knowing firsthand how challenging it is to build a real estate investing business from scratch, we created DPI to be a partnering cooperative with investors who couldn't seem to get over the hump. We created a partnering/affiliate program where promising investors could leverage the partners experience and connections to build their own business.

It is the next generation of real estate investing; taking mentoring/coaching and creating a win/win partnership to help those who are struggling to achieve their goal of financial freedom through real estate.

You probably know us as wholesalers. We love that you know us as wholesalers. We are happy to share our knowledge & information to help you do wholesale deals. In case you haven't read it yet, our first book is titled, "The Ultimate Guide To Wholesaling Real Estate." It can be bought on Amazon. We also have a ton of material on www.FreeWholesaleCourse.com. That is our pride and joy. We have put a lot of information out there for the world. Right now, we've got over 10,000 students. We have hundreds of positive reviews. When somebody asks us out to coffee (to pick our brain), it's our way of leveraging our time. We ask them to check out our course first. Once we're on the same page, we'd be happy to meet up and chat. We want to get everyone caught up to speed on what wholesaling is.

This book, however, is about acquiring a massive rental property portfolio with little to no money out of pocket. We'll share our strategies, and tricks we picked up along the way. For more information, videos, and forms, we also have the website www.FreeLandlordCourse.com.

David A. Dodge

A bootstrapping, serial entrepreneur and ninja coach/mentor. While attending the University of Missouri, in 2005, one of David's professors introduced him to the book "Rich Dad Poor Dad" by Robert Kiyosaki which planted the entrepreneurial seed.

After graduating in 2007, David did a series of jobs from sales for a fortune 500 company to traveling the country with CNN covering the 2008 Presidential Election. All the time thinking about "Rich Dad Poor Dad", the entrepreneurial itch grew stronger and had to be seriously scratched.

With tens of thousands of dollars in credit card debt and sick of working for other people, David made the leap, quit his job and became a full-time real estate investor. With mounting debt and no source of income he was in a "succeed or go broke" situation – failure was not an option.

Learning from trial by fire, David made every mistake in the book as he built his real estate portfolio. Focusing on his end goal of financial freedom, he pushed through the failures and setbacks to build a thriving business.

As of today, David has ownership in over 65 rental properties however wholesaling is his favorite way to make quick money. He also leverages wholesaling as a way to cherry pick the deals to find rehab and flip deals or add to his portfolio of rental properties.

Being a serial entrepreneur, David also has several other successful business ventures in ecommerce and cyber currency investing. Now David Dodge is St. Louis Real Estate Investor with over 15 years of experience. He first started investing in Real Estate when he was 21 years old. He was still in college at the University of Missouri-Columbia. David specializes in wholesaling properties as well as teaching others how to wholesale Real Estate for huge profits.

David and his team averages about 8-12 wholesales a month and have wholesaled over 500 houses to date with his company "House Sold Easy" (a division of DPI). David also loves to fix-and-flip properties as well as add properties to his rental portfolio. David has over 65 rentals currently and he has a goal to build his rental portfolio to over 150 properties in the next 24-36 months. You can follow him on Instagram to find out more about his journey to "150 houses". He shows images of each property as well as how much rent he collects on each property.

Mike Slane

Bad ass marketer and the Navy Seal of building business systems. Having a Master of Business Administration degree, and to paraphrase Tina Turner, Mike got a good job in the city, working for the man every night and day. Also greatly influenced by "Rich Dad Poor Dad", he had a strong yearning to leave corporate America and achieve financial freedom through passive income.

Mike started his real estate investing career in 2009. He purchased a four-family apartment building. It was his first home as he moved into one of the units and was the landlord on duty. House Hacking before it was cool! This strategy is known as a "House Hack" today because the rental payments from the other units cover the expenses of his unit. By reducing his monthly expenses, and living within his means, he eventually achieved his goal of living off passive income. He began adding a few more rentals to his portfolio and expanded his means. By 2016 he quit his day job working for The Man! He was able to work full time for himself in Real Estate. He began wholesaling real estate to increase his income, meanwhile growing his rental portfolio. Though he enjoyed the financial freedom real estate offered, he quickly realized that he did not want to be a property manager.

Utilizing his MBA, he developed a systemized process to invest in rental properties and outsource the property management. Realizing he didn't want to wait until he was 65 to retire, Mike quit his job as an insurance underwriter and became a full-time real estate investor.

Though he had some income from his rental property it wasn't nearly enough to sustain any kind of lifestyle. As Mike says, "I wasn't living a luxurious lifestyle. I had just enough to pay the bills and that was it."

Not having extra cash to invest, Mike focused on doing wholesale deals. It took him six months to get his first deal under his belt. The initial six months were filled with doubt and fear. Mike was second guessing if he had made the right decision.

But once he got the first deal done, it made the second one easier and quicker. Then the third was even faster, and the fourth was even faster and so on. Having experienced firsthand the struggle to start a real estate investing business from scratch, Mike came up with DPI's partnering/mentor concept to leverage his knowledge and experience to help struggling investors achieve financial freedom and began searching out successful real estate investors who'd be a good fit to partner with on this hybrid business structure. When he teamed up with the other Discount Property investors is when he really began to leverage the BRRRR strategy and explode his and their portfolio growth.

Bill Maret

Visionary and endless idea man. Bill is the old timer of DPI. Working for corporate America for 25 years in the high-tech industry, Bill was the go-to guy in outside sales and business development.

Being at the top of his profession Bill was enjoying all the benefits that come from being in the top 5% of earners in the world. But he soon realized that when you work for someone else, they always expect more. Plus, there is always some young gun looking to take you down.

Though he was making great money, the long hours, stress, and continued management press to beat last year's success took its toll. The big house, summer home, boats, and all the other toys couldn't get rid of the bad case of "corporate burnout" Bill was experiencing.

Like David and Mike, Bill read "Rich Dad Poor Dad" and it showed him a way out of the corporate insane asylum. Even though he was over 50, Bill knew it was time to take action toward true freedom.

He started his real estate investing in 2006. When the housing market crashed, Bill saw an opportunity to accelerate his business.

Unlike David and Mike, Bill took a slower and more strategic approach. He continued to work his job while building his portfolio. After about a decade of acquiring rental properties, Bill was able to generate enough passive income to say adios to corporate America forever and become his own boss. Whereas David and Mike used wholesaling to generate quick cash, Bill leveraged wholesalers as a source to find good deals and would buy properties from them.

Bill is our third partner. He does more of the behind the scenes work with the rest of the team. Bill has a long history of corporate experience. He decided the corporate gig was not for him. In less than 2 years he took massive action and replaced his high paying corporate salary with rental properties. His corporate experience translated into efficient business planning. He uses a strategy known as the "GOSPA". He's the planning guru for the team. GOSPA stands for Goals, Objectives, Strategy, Plans, Action. It's a great planning technique for accomplishing big goals. He was the original proponent in the group of leveraging the BRRRR strategy for the group, after he successfully leveraged it himself.

The Team

Together David, Mike, and Bill make up the backbone of Discount Property Investors. Utilizing their collective experience, knowledge and expertise to mentor, coach and partner with other investors to build one of the largest and fastest growing real estate investing companies.

CHAPTER 2

What Is BRRRR?

We love wholesaling, but we also see it as a job. What we're passionate about now is building a portfolio of rental properties for ourselves. We're really excited about what we're doing, and the way we're doing it. We did not invent this method. We're just following a model that we want to share with you. That model is affectionately known as BRRRR. Buy, Rehab, Rent, Refinance, and Repeat.

There are only five key components to the BRRRR model. Below is an overview of each component. Each component will be broken down to more rigorous detail in later chapters.

Five Key Components:

- Buying
- Rehab

- Rent

- Refinance

- Repeat

Buying

Buying property can be broken down into three aspects. Finding the property, analyzing the property, and funding the property.

One of our favorite sayings about Real Estate is, "This is not Rocket Science". That is a joke our friend and mentor likes to make. He was a rocket scientist in a former life and can testify that this really is not that complicated by comparison. No matter where you live there is almost a 100% chance you can find a rental property nearby. Someone else is renting property around you, so you can too. It doesn't matter where you live or where you want to invest. That said, there are a couple things to keep in mind when buying a property using the BRRRR strategy.

Before you buy a property, you need to figure out what type of property is going to make sense for you. It's best to "begin with the end in mind" to be successful in BRRRR investing. Figure out what area has rents that will support the mortgage and expenses. We suggest starting local. Go to local investment clubs and find out what other people are doing in your area. Why re-invent the wheel? Other investors will tell you which areas are hot and which areas to avoid. Pay attention to what other landlords are doing. Success leaves clues.

We also suggest lining up your funding before looking for houses to buy. Banks can help you define your buying criteria by knowing what they will and won't lend on. Also, it would be a waste of time to shop around for houses, to find out you don't qualify in the first place. The great thing about BRRRR is you get to use and re-use and re-use the same funds over and over. You won't need millions of dollars to create a multi-million-dollar portfolio. When we started, we had access to around $300,000 in private funds. We turned that modest sum of money into a portfolio of cash flowing rentals. Now we currently have around 100 doors (units), with a market value of approximately $10,000,000. By the time this book is published, we will be at our 150 doors mark and around $15,000,000.

There are a couple of different options for funding the initial purchase. Later in the book we discuss the pros and cons of each option. The most common options are cash, a line of credit, traditional bank financing, or private funding. Private Money is our preferred method because it is quick and easy. If you don't have enough cash or good enough credit to buy a house, it's very possible to talk to a friend or family member about and ask them if they'd be willing to loan you money for an investment property. It's a win-win situation for the lender and the borrower. The money loan is backed by the property, which makes it a fairly secure investment compared to other investments. As the borrower, you can negotiate interest rates with the private lender. Private funding allows you to close on a house quicker and with less hassle than some of the other options.

When you have an idea of where to look and you have funding in place, you'll want to go out and actually find a property. One option is buying property off the MLS (Multiple

Listing Service). Our preferred method though is buying off market. We gained traction in real estate via wholesaling. We buy unlisted properties at a discount from motivated sellers and resell them for a profit. We think it's the best way to find and negotiate deals. For more information, check out www.FreeWholesaleCourse.com. It is possible to buy great deals from the MLS, with the help of a good agent. However, it's not our preferred method.

Analyzing a property to make sure it meets your buying criteria is probably the most important step in the BRRRR strategy. Deal analysis can be a make or break for you, especially when leveraging your money. We use a simple spreadsheet to help us analyze every property before we buy it. (See figure 1). We start with the purchase price, then the rehab cost, then the after-repair value (ARV), and the estimated rent. We'll share with you how we go about getting these numbers later. However, for now, we just want you to have an overview of the process. Once you have these numbers in place, you can figure out what your cash flow will be based on the current mortgage rates. This also gives a good idea of how much money we can pull out of the property. We want to pull all of our money back out, while still having around 20% equity. We suggest setting up a spreadsheet like this to help you analyze the numbers. The numbers don't lie. No need to overthink it or get emotional about buying a property. Enter the numbers into the spreadsheet, and you'll know if you have a deal or not. Our sheet

Property Address : BE A DISCOUNT PROPERY INVESTOR	
Purchase Price	$85,000
Rehab + Holding Cost	$7,000
Property Value (Estimated ARV)	$130,000
Estimated Monthly Rent	$1,200
Rehab Contingency (10%)	$700
Estimated All in Price	$92,700
Estimated Mortgage Amount	$97,500
Estimated Interest Rate	5.00%
Estimated Amortization (Years)	20
Loan to Value REFI% (70% - 80%)	75%
Estimated Mortgage Payment (P+I)	$643
Estimated Insurance and Taxes	$150
Estimated Property Mgt	$96
Total Monthly Estimated Cost	$889
Expected Cash Back at REFI % ^^	**$4,800**
Expected CashFlow per Month	**$311**
Expected Equity or sale profit	**$32,500**

is pretty slick. We type in the first 4 numbers (purchase price, repair costs, ARV, and rent). The last 3 rows give us all the information we need to decide if a deal works or not. We want to get our cash back by refinancing. We'll also know our expected cash flow and expected equity capture. Get a copy of this sheet at www.FreeLandlordCourse.com.

Rehabbing

When you think of rehabbing, you're probably thinking of those house flipping shows on tv. Some of those projects could be overwhelming to a new investor. The good news is, rehabbing for a rental does not have to be as extensive or as costly! There are two big reasons to rehab your rentals. First, if you're buying properties at a discount, they're almost always distressed or outdated. Second, by adding value to the property you open up the possibility of earning the "entrepreneurial credit". This allows you to get more money out of a property than you put into it when you refinance with a bank.

The good news is you do not have to be handy to do this. We rarely do any work on our properties ourselves, we don't need "sweat equity". If anything, spending a little more money by having a professional do the work helps us. We put less stress on our bodies and get more time to look for more deals. Plus, they're the professionals that know what they're doing. We hire contractors we trust. We'll give you tips on how to interview and hire handymen; plus, how to communicate with and manage them too.

Renting

Renting out properties can seem daunting at first, but it's really no big deal if you treat it like a business. It doesn't matter if you have 1 rental or 100 rentals in your portfolio, it's important to treat each tenant like a customer. You owe your customers a certain level of service, especially if you want to keep them. On the flipside, customers have certain responsibilities. They need to respect your property and pay rent on time or you can't afford to keep them as a customer anymore. If you're managing your properties yourself, you have to have this mentality. If you don't maintain a high level of professionalism, you'll likely be walked all over by professional tenants, and/or your good tenants will move out for greener pastures.

The best way to handle tenants is to be proactive about finding and screening tenants. Finding and keeping a good tenant through a rigorous screening process is far easier than dealing with a problem tenant later. With the advent of the internet and new technologies, finding good tenants has changed so much and yet stayed the same. One of our favorite methods for finding tenants was using a yard sign. It's still very helpful, but we also publish all of our rentals online too. Our goal is to get our properties rented to qualified tenants quickly. There's a lot of amazing tools for screening potential tenants and collecting rent.

It's also SUPER important to get your property rented quickly. By doing this, you'll reduce holding costs, and most banks require the property to be rented out prior to refinancing with them. Having a property rented with a solid lease helps get your money back.

Maintenance is a critical component of owning rental property. It's also a big reason why many people don't want to own rental properties. People dread the 2 am maintenance call that a toilet is leaking into the basement. We've managed hundreds of properties for years and it is very rare to get that type of emergency call. We utilize preventive maintenance in our rehabs. However, when we do get a call, it can be a challenge but it's not the end of the world. The occasional maintenance call is not going to keep us from building a portfolio of rentals. We wanted to free ourselves from our day jobs. We hope you have the same attitude.

As you grow your portfolio, you can turn your properties over to a professional property manager. When you do that is entirely up to you. However, we suggest you manage your properties until you have at least 6-10 units for a handful of reasons. We'll discuss how to find, screen, and manage your property managers. Yes, you will need to manage your managers. They're not mind readers and might have different goals than you. We'll show you what to watch out for, and how to utilize them to give yourself more freedom.

Refinancing

Refinancing is the name of the game when it comes to the BRRRR strategy. This goes for if you're just getting started or if you're a seasoned investor. We refinance properties all the time. At this time (2019-2020) we're experiencing an especially low interest rate environment. The money we can borrow is cheap, relatively speaking. We say that this is the most important step in BRRRR model, because you need to refinance to get your money out of the property. Without doing so, it would be impossible to do the final "R" in this strategy, REPEAT. Pulling your money out allows you to buy more properties quickly. It's so important we almost feel like we should rename the BRRRR acronym and call it the PBRRRR method. The letter "P" standing for **P**requalify with a lender. Refinancing is a must for this method. Banks traditionally have the cheapest money to borrow, which is where you should refinance your properties.

It's great, it's really not even money out of your pocket because the tenants pay that note for you. So, find a local bank and tell them how you want to invest in real estate using the BRRRR method. If a bank tells you "no", keep going to other local banks until you find one that will approve you. If you can't get approved, make sure you're listening to why they can't approve you. Figure out what you need to fix with your finances so you can get approved. Chances are, you need to improve your credit score, lower your debt to income ratio, or you might need to get a cosigner. Take the time to get a relationship with a banker before you dive into the deep end of BRRRR.

Repeat

This is where the magic happens again and again and again! By refinancing and getting your cash (or private money) back, you can now use it to acquire another rental property. If you're working full time and 'playing' in real estate part time, then doing one project at a time a few times a year can still turn into a sizable rental portfolio in a few years. The average person can use the same hundred thousand dollars again and again to build a multi-million-dollar portfolio. Below is a quick example of the snowball effect of reusing your money to acquire assets. If you buy, rehab, and refinance 2 properties a year. For this example, we're assuming a $20k equity capture. This occurs by buying right, sticking to a rehab budget, and getting the appraisal/refinance to allow for you to pull all your invested money out. We'll also assume $0 in asset appreciation, $100K property value (after rehab), $80K loans, and $400/month net cash flow.

Year 1

1st Purchase - 20K Equity, $0 in property, $400/month cash flow

2nd Property - 20K Equity, $0 in property, $400/month cash flow

Year 2

1st Purchase - 20K Equity, $0 in property, $400/month cash flow

2nd Property - 20K Equity, $0 in property, $400/month cash flow

Year 3

1st Purchase - 20K Equity, $0 in property, $400/month cash flow

2nd Property - 20K Equity, $0 in property, $400/month cash flow

This is possible by just doing 2 projects a year using the same $100K you have available from private money, cash reserves, or line of credit.

After 3 years, that's a total of $120K in equity and $2400/month in cash flow that you created without leaving any money in the portfolio.

After 5 years, that's a total of $200K in equity and $4,000/month in cash flow.

After 10 years, that's a total of $400K in equity and $8,000/month in cash flow. This doesn't even include any

APPRECIATION on the properties. We consider appreciation just icing on the cake. We hope that gets you excited!

BRRRR vs. Wholesaling vs. Rehabber

Which strategy is right for you? Let's briefly look at the mindset of the investor in each of the following strategies; Wholesaler, Rehabber, and Rental Investor (buy and hold).

The wholesaler is someone that is going to look for decent chunks of money quickly. Typically, wholesalers are newer to real estate investing, although there's plenty of seasoned investors who still do wholesaling. They like to "run and gun". They tend to be extroverted and enjoy quick sales. This is where we recommend most people start investing. Wholesaling allows you to gain knowledge about rehab numbers and comps (comparable properties) without putting your own money on the line. Check out our first book "The Ultimate Guide to Wholesaling Real Estate" to learn everything you need to know and more about this strategy. We also have the online course www.FreeWholesaleCourse.com. A wholesaler buys at a great price and sells at a good price. They're typically not selling to the general public, but rather other real estate investors. These investors are either rental buyers or rehabbers. These investors will look at a deal and provide the wholesaler feedback on whether the numbers work or not. This is why we suggest starting here when it comes to real estate investing. The quick cash, low risk, and ability to gain experience quickly make it a great place to start.

The rehabber is typically a more experienced investor. They're good with project management and handling budgets. This person is willing to make larger chunks of money a bit more slowly. They tend to be creative people and can manage risk.

The rental investor will typically look at things from a long-term perspective. They tend to be more analytical by nature. The saying, "Slow and steady wins the race," best describes the buy and hold investor. They know they're not going to get rich quickly by purchasing 1 or 2 houses a year. However, they plan on building long term wealth slowly. All investments have risk. However, income producing properties bought at a discount and managed well is our favorite way to build wealth.

Recap: What Is BRRRR?

1. **Buying:** Determine your business model, and what types of properties work for you. Then find and fund the purchase of them.

2. **Rehabbing:** Rehabbing a property is necessary because most properties are in need of repair when buying at a discount. Rehabbing helps get a higher appraisal and is useful for preventative maintenance.

3. **Renting:** Getting a property occupied is how you make money in this business and is often necessary for refinancing.

4. **Refinancing:** Refinancing is the name of the game. It allows you to pull your money out to reinvest in acquiring other assets. Get pre-qualified first.

5. **Repeating:** Utilize the snowball effect. You'll acquire more properties and experience over time on your journey to freedom.

BRRRR is a great strategy because it will allow you to use little to none of your own money. You use private investor's money, or hard money lenders to purchase properties. Then get these properties set up as assets that cash flow and pay you money every month. Then you get a bank loan to refinance you out of that hard money or your private money loan. Then you have a loan with a bank for a long period of time at a low interest rate. It allows you to purchase lots of assets in a quick way with using little to none of your own money. We have purchased 100 properties using this method over the past 2 years and continue to utilize this strategy

Action Item: Start meeting with local bankers to get pre-approved for loans. You'll gain knowledge and experience from their expertise. Plus, refinancing is a critical part of the BRRRR model. You want to be prequalified when it's time to refinance to avoid any major hiccups. This will also give you a sense of how much money you'll make in cash flow and how much equity you can pull out after a rehab. This is handy information for establishing buying criteria and budgets.

"Failing to Plan is planning to fail." -Alan Lakein

CHAPTER 3

When & Why of BRRRR

Before we go into the specifics of the BRRRR method you need to remember what your goal is here? It should be FREEDOM! Freedom from the 9-5, financial freedom, freedom to live life on you your terms. Real Estate has made more people millionaires than any other side hustle. You might make some extra cash selling essential oils or vitamin gummies but you most likely aren't going to create a lifestyle of freedom or build generational wealth. You have to determine what freedom is to you? Is it an extra $1000/month, is it $10K/month, or $100K/month?

Owning rental real estate can do this for you. It's not the sexy BIG paydays with little to no money out of pocket like wholesaling. It is, however, the slow proven way to wealth. That is the real Sexy! You get rental Income, you get to depreciate your properties (tax write offs), you get appreciation (gain value) in the property, you get to leverage other people's money, you get someone else (tenants) to buy you something really expensive. If you are out there looking for a quick buck, then wholesaling is for you. That is a great way to generate those chunks of much needed cash. It is a job though. However, if you're looking for freedom, then buy income producing rental properties. What do you hope to achieve? Do you want financial freedom or a little extra money each month? Then go after rentals for cash flow. If you want to retire your wife or yourself, then go after rentals.

We (The Discount Property Investors) are going after 150 single family rental properties. That would be 50 Doors a piece. Even if we ignore appreciation and rent increases, we should achieve $20K/month in net cash flow and 1.0MM in equity. We all agreed that this is enough for us all to achieve financial freedom. It seemed like a good number to shoot for, then we are going to split up. We wanted to begin with the end in mind. Our goal is to do this in 3 years. We are currently about ⅔ of the way through this goal when we saw the market heating up and decided to sell some rentals for much larger profits than we thought should be available. So, we slowed down on this goal...for now!

We are really just managing our portfolio now, and the number of doors seems to fluctuate. If there is too much equity in your hands that is an opportunity for someone else to try and take it. By this, we mean that people get greedy, and you could get sued. This is another reason we like refinancing - or equity stripping. We would rather owe money on the assets than own them free and clear. We will get to 150 when the time is right for us. We continue to add rentals and sell off turnkeys right now while the market is strong. But we also like to add cash flowing rentals. It's all a numbers game. This is very similar to our mindset about wholesaling; create win-win relationships and know your numbers. We buy distressed properties and fix them up, we bring them new life and give a tenant (individuals or families) nice places to live. We are extremely responsive to tenants when maintenance issues arise. We try to do as much preventative maintenance as possible when doing our rehabs. We want to have nice houses, and a nice place for our tenants to live. We view them as clients.

We don't know what your freedom number is, and you probably don't either at this moment. But we'll delve into that later. Most people get into real estate because of their desire for freedom. However, those people quickly find out there is no freedom in real estate. It's not too long before they find out that real estate involves a lot of hard work. You're constantly busting your ass to get a deal and make money. That's fine though. If it was easy, everyone would do it. We also tend to appreciate things more when we have to work hard to obtain them as opposed to if we were just given them. This is why it's so important to dive deep and establish a strong, motivating why. Because it does get tough sometimes, but it's worth it.

Rental properties are a way to invest in real estate to get freedom. Most people don't understand the connection there. You obtain freedom through rentals. It might not be freedom today, but it will give you freedom later in life if you work it right. If you own enough rental properties, you can obtain freedom. It's all dependent on maximizing cash flow and systemizing your business like anything else, which we'll teach you. Passive income is also taxed less than active income. We love that someone else is paying off our assets for us. We love the freedom to work for ourselves. We love our time freedom, and lifestyle.

Mike used to consider himself lazy. Then he realized that he's not really lazy. In fact, he likes doing stuff and having a purpose. He thought that once he had enough passive income, he'd do nothing. He came to realize that it wasn't that he wanted to do nothing, but rather gain time freedom. He wanted the freedom to do what he wanted to do when we wanted to do it. Time freedom is the new wealthy. It's not being rich. It's true wealth.

Mike had bills paid. Now he wants to keep upping that number. He doesn't want to have to report to a boss or have to find that next deal. We like finding deals. We enjoy it. But we don't have to, that's the real why. We want multigenerational wealth, so our families don't have to work. It's fun to have mental stimulation. Routines are healthy. We'll never "retire". If you position yourself as an investor, talking to people and walking through properties is fun. We're not breaking our backs working. If you're over 30, you shouldn't be swinging a hammer. That's our motto. It's ridiculous, 30 isn't that old, and many people work construction far later into life. It's hard work, and we don't want to do it. We don't, because we don't have to. That's what we mean by freedom. Making ourselves happy is our number one intention. Pretty often, your 'why' will come down to the same couple of things for you.

We use a process we learned from the book, "Start With Why" by Simon Sinek. We just keep asking ourselves "Why?" until we get to our root motivation. Ask yourself "Why do you want to own rental property?" Then keep drilling down on that 'why'. We want to own rental property because it's passive income. "Why is this important?" We get to work less, and we get taxed less. "Why is this important?" We can keep more of our money and have more time freedom. "Why is this important?" We can do what we want to do when we want to do it. "Why is that important?" Because it makes us happy. When you can't drill down any further, that's your true why.

If happiness, and freedom are valuable to you, then you found the right book. Those are our core motivations, and we'll share our process of how you can do the same. Everything that happens, happens in the present moment by the choices you make. So, start NOW!

Action Item: Find your 'why'. Ask yourself, "Why do I want to own rental properties? Or why did I choose to start reading this book? Write down your answers, and keep asking yourself "Why is that important to me?" After you ask yourself several times, and you can't simplify your answer anymore, you've found your true motivation. Your fundamental "Why."

"The two most important days of your life are the day you were born, and the day you find out why." -Mark Twain

CHAPTER 4

Why Rentals?

There are so many reasons to buy rentals if you're trying to generate extra income and build wealth. As a reader of this book, you're probably already interested in acquiring rentals, and aware of some of the benefits. However, we want to discuss some of the reasons we LOVE buying and owning rentals:

Benefits Owning Rental Property:

- Cash Flow
- Good Debt (somebody else paying down your mortgage)
- Leverage
- Appreciation
- Tax Benefits
- Wealth Creation

Cash Flow

There are a lot of ways to calculate cash flow. We'll talk about how we do it, and how other people do it. We just like to keep it simple. There is no reason to over complicate anything. When we look at our cash flow, we use a little formula. We take what we think the property is going to rent for, then we subtract the cost of the mortgage, which has our insurance and taxes built into it. Then we also subtract our property management fee, and also set aside money for vacancy and maintenance. We usually set aside about 10% of the gross income for the vacancy and maintenance reserves. That's how we calculate cash flow. It's easy, and that's what is important to us.

To look at this from the 10,000 ft. view, we think of cash flow as the difference between all your monthly expenses and your rental income. We want to stress though, it's really important to include all the little expenses, because they can add up. Sometimes those costs aren't even a cost, but rather a lack of income, hence vacancy.

Good Debt vs. Bad Debt

We want to leverage our money out as much as possible. Right now, it's cheap money. We want to get as much of it as we can. Our goal is to get in as much debt as we can. However, it's good debt, not bad debt. We first heard this concept through the book, "Rich Dad, Poor Dad." By Robert Kiyosaki. Bad debt is debt that we have to pay. That's how we look at it. Good debt is debt that someone else pays for. We're paying it off, but we're not working for that money to pay it off, we're just waiting. We're trading time for wealth. We mentioned earlier, people are taxed on their income, not so much when they create wealth. The name of the game is to create wealth.

Robert Kiyosaki describes at length the difference between good debt and bad debt. Good debt is used to pay for assets. Assets are any investments that put money back into our pockets. Rental properties are a great asset. On the flip side, bad debt is referred to as consumer debt. This can be credit card payments, or car payments. Even the mortgage on your house would be considered bad debt in his eyes. This is where he makes the distinction between assets and liabilities. A house is a liability because you're paying for it, rather than it making money for you. Most people think of owning a home as their biggest asset. However, when you really understand the difference between an asset and a liability, you'll know it's actually a liability. Learn the difference between asset and liability. Learn the difference between good debt and bad debt.

Leverage

We love rentals because we can leverage the money we use to buy them. You can't really walk into a bank and say, "I want to borrow 100K and I'm going to invest that money into Microsoft and Apple stock." You can try, but they're going to say no every time. It doesn't work that way. Maybe, you could use a credit card, and get a cash advance to invest. The main point is that owning a share of stock in a major Fortune 500 company should be considered a pretty significant asset. However, banks are not comfortable lending you the money to purchase a stock like that. Banks don't care about it. However, banks do lend on real estate which is good for us. We think this is because real estate is a real asset. It's something tangible. It's unique. These companies can issue more stock; however, you can't create more land; unless you live in Dubai. All jokes aside, you can't build more land, and there is only so much United States of America. They can't make more of it. Banks use that real property as collateral, and they'll loan to you on it. Sometimes they'll loan up to 100% of what you have invested.

A great way to leverage your money is through a conventional mortgage. To make the math easy, we'll talk about using a $100,000 home for this example. If you wanted to buy that property, you could put all $100,000 into that property. However, you would have zero leverage on it. You'd have all your money tied up, and none of anyone else's. However, with a conventional loan, you usually bring 20% to the table, or 20% down. Of that $100,000 house, you'd only have to bring $20,000. That means you'd still have $80,000 in your pocket to either spend or invest compared to buying the house outright for $100,000. You can acquire an asset for a small percentage of what you'd actually have to pay if you didn't leverage your money. Somebody else is helping pay for it.

With this $100,000 example, we can then go out and buy four more houses with that same money. We'd be financing the other 80% on each one. We'd be controlling half a million dollars' worth of assets with our $100,000. This is what we mean by 'leverage'. Hopefully you can now see how powerful it is to leverage your money. That's what we do with real estate, especially when markets are going up.

Appreciation

We like to maintain the property and keep it in the same condition if not better. That way, when we sell it, we get to take advantage of the appreciation. Appreciation just means that we're able to sell the house for more than we bought it for. We don't let our houses fall apart. We have to keep the maintenance up for appreciation to even be a factor. That house needs to be in good condition when we sell it. If it's falling apart or deteriorating from lack of maintenance, we wouldn't expect it to go up in value. We buy houses like that all the time. There isn't any appreciation because they've let those houses go. That's how we find deals. We find people who have let their houses go. However, if we maintain the house properly, the value of that house will most likely increase along with the market.

The value of the house will increase for several reasons. One reason would be inflation in general. When the dollar has a lower buying power, things typically cost more. Therefore, at a later date, these houses will generally have more value. Another reason a property might appreciate is the scarcity of land. There's only so much land to build on. So being closer to metro areas, shopping, good school districts, etc., make land a scarce and valuable resource. We're sure you've heard the phrase, "Location, Location, Location."

The National Association of Realtors (NAR) published some data about the rising prices of homes. From 1968 until about 2004, the average price of owning a home increased about 6.5% during this period. They said there wasn't a single year of decline. So historically housing prices have gone up steadily, even more than inflation. We're all aware of what happened in 2007-2008. We had that bubble and a big crash. Since then, we saw the real estate market stumble, then it picked up again.

From 1968-2004, a 36-year period, the market had a steady 6.5% gain. We don't actually plan on our assets appreciating, so that 6.5% is just a bonus to us. We buy properties that cash flow regardless of housing prices. That is our favorite part of it. The appreciation is really just icing on the cake. That's a shout out to Jason Hartman. We like his "Creating Wealth Podcast". We'll throw him a little plug here. That's what he says, "Cash flow is key, appreciation is the icing on the cake". We couldn't agree more. That's the way we look at it as well. We don't think about appreciation when making a purchase, because it is not guaranteed. And we have little control over it. However, when we do get appreciation on a property, that added value is a pretty sweet icing on the cake.

Tax Benefits

Let's talk about the tax benefits. There are multiple tax benefits you can take advantage of when owning rental properties. You don't really get those tax benefits when you are wholesaling. Wholesaling is great for generating a good chunk of change. We all want that. Everybody loves a good pay day. But after you collect that money, you're going to have to pay income taxes on that for the most part.

Here we'll explain what tax deductions you can use for owning real estate, and how they benefit you. The biggest tax deduction is going to be your interest on your loan. Most people are buying rentals with mortgages on them. That's what we do, and that's what we teach our students to do as well. All the interest that you pay to the bank or the mortgage company, you can write that off as a deduction on your taxes. All the repairs that you make on that home you can write those off. If you are travelling to and from that property, you can write that off. You can write off a small portion of your home that you live in if you have a home office. We're not tax attorneys or accountants. We are just giving you information that we've used to our advantage. Once you get into real estate your taxes get more complicated, so you probably need to start working with a CPA to help guide you. This is a good thing because you are likely making more money and taking more tax deductions.

The other biggest tax deduction in our opinion is kind of a hidden one. It's called depreciation. In the United States, where we live, we can depreciate property over a 27.5-year period. Depreciation is a reduction in the value of an asset with the passage of time, due in particular to wear and tear. This is a unique expense. We didn't necessarily pay anything out of your pocket; however, we can deduct this "expense" from our taxes.

For example, if you bought a $100k house, the IRS is essentially saying that it will be worth $0 or have outlived its "useful life" at the end of 27.5 years. Why the IRS chose 27.5 years instead of anything else is beyond us. It's probably because two lawmakers argued over how long it should be, one said 25, one said 30, and they said let's meet in the middle. To determine depreciation, you take the cost of the property and the money invested (repairs, etc.) into that property. Then you divide that value by 27.5. You get to deduct that amount every year from your taxes. If you took that $100k house and divided its value out over 27.5 years, you'd get around $3600 worth of tax deductions!! These deductions really stack up when you multiply them by using leverage to buy more houses the way we mentioned before.

Owning rental properties can give you a handful of useful deductions too. You can deduct mortgage interest, repairs, travel, a home office, and depreciation etc. So why is that important? Let's say the income on the property was less than those deductions. You can then offset other income you make by owning real estate. Rental property can actually save you money in taxes rather than increase it. So, it's an asset that not only makes you wealthy over time, but if you do it right, it can actually save you money on your taxes just by owning it. Remember, a penny saved is a penny earned.

These are laws that are written into the IRS tax code. They're basically telling you how to avoid paying taxes. There are 73,954 pages of tax code. And here's a little secret, only about five of those pages tell you when, where, and how you need to pay those taxes. Everything else is a law on how to defer taxes or to avoid them altogether. We're not avoiding taxes to cheat the government. These laws were created by the government as an incentive structure.

All this tax stuff can get pretty complicated and is going to be somewhat unique to your personal situation and tax strategy. We strongly advise that you seek the advice of a CPA to help you with this. We're not professionals at this part of the real estate game, we have CPA's. We have multiple CPA's. We're trying to give you a feel for the tax benefits of owning real estate in general. It's one of the big reasons why we like real estate. CPA's are a critical part of your team, and they help us do what we do.

Wealth Creation

It's our opinion that taxes were written and created by the rich to protect the rich. That's the only reason we have taxes. Now, taxes are used by the government to help support the infrastructure. However, knowing the origin of taxes, it now makes sense that the government taxes income. This is very important. We're not saying that this is right or wrong, but rather, our observation of reality. We can't really change the tax code; however, we can do our best to understand and benefit from these tax laws. The government taxes income, they do not tax wealth! If you're able to create wealth, you don't really pay taxes on the wealth creation. However, if you want to sell that wealth, then you'll receive an income. That income is what's taxed. We hope this makes sense. Take full advantage of the tax benefits of owning real estate, and become wealthy!

Not everybody understands the freedom aspect. Once, we were refinancing some of our rental properties with one of the bankers we use. He was happy to do business with us. He had already done about 10 to 15 loans with us at the time. Then on a recently acquired rental property, he seemed concerned that we were "not getting rich off this one". We just sat there and smiled. We replied, "You're absolutely right, but we own over 40 of them." The goal for our company is to own 150 rental properties, then split up our assets. Every partner will own 50 doors (units) each. We'll each have about $20K/month in passive income and over $1 million in equity, and a portfolio value of around $5 million. So yes, that banker was right. We're not getting rich off any one property overnight. However, over time, we are building massive wealth.

We're not trying to get rich off this. It's not a get rich quick scheme. Our goal is to become *wealthy* over the next 15 years. It's a mindset that most people don't quite understand. Rich is just having a lot of cash in the bank or the ability to spend a lot of cash. A million dollars

> *"We'd rather be wealthy than rich"*

in the bank may make someone 'rich' in today's dollars, but it won't make them wealthy. That money can be spent in a relatively short period of time. Depending on the person, it might take a few years. It certainly wouldn't last a lifetime for most people. Riches disappear. Wealth is sustainable. Wealth is about owning assets that produce income for you. That can be businesses or income producing assets like rental properties. It would take a long time to spend wealth, because that money keeps coming in. Rich is just having a lot of money. However, wealth is about sustainability. We plan on being wealthy for the rest of our lives. To us, that house represents $300/month of cash flow. It takes time. It's not going to make us rich but rather *wealthy*. It's going to buy us freedom. That $300 keeps coming every month. Then we'll receive even more once we pay off the loan. It's so exciting.

We love rentals. On the path to freedom, one rental won't cut it. It'll probably be more like ten. If you can have ten rentals paid off, then you're really going to be rocking it.

There's a quote, "Real estate is the number one asset that has created more wealth and more millionaires than anything else." That's why real estate is so exciting to us.

Remember, you're not taxed on wealth creation, you're really only taxed on income. By deferring the loan payments, someone else is paying down the debt you have. You're adding to your wealth versus income. It's also a guaranteed way to save. Each house is essentially a small piggy bank when you buy it. Over the 10 to 15 years the debt is being paid down, it's as though it's a piggy bank as big as a car filled with hundred-dollar bills. It's awesome! The tax benefits, the leverage of increasing your cash on cash return, the property value going up, and creating extra money through cash flow are all factors that make rental property great for the wealth creation. That's why we do it. It's all a part of wealth creation, which leads us to freedom. We work hard now, to have freedom later. Freedom. That's the name of the game. That's the direction we're headed. We can't wait to have 150 piggy banks the size of cars working for us.

A 1031 exchange is also a huge tax benefit of owning rental property. As we mentioned, you get to deduct depreciation over the course of 27.5 years. However, you'll have to pay those tax savings back when you sell a property, because it's considered income at that point. You can save yourself money by doing a 1031 exchange. You sell that property and buy another asset with that money. This resets the basis (value). Now you'll have another 27.5 years to deduct depreciation, if you buy more rental property. The basis also resets when property is inherited.

Recap:

1. **Cash Flow:** This is the surplus of money we get by subtracting our expenses from our gross revenue. We intend to cash flow around $300-400 per property per month.

2. **Good Debt Vs. Bad Debt:** Good debt is used to acquire assets. The debt is paid down by somebody else. Bad

debt is consumer debt like car payments, credit card debt, and even your primary residence. These are considered liabilities.

3. **Leverage:** We can acquire assets like rental property by utilizing banks and using a fraction of our own money.

4. **Appreciation:** Properties tend to go up in value if properly maintained. We don't assume this is the case, but it's icing on the cake when it happens.

5. **Tax Benefits:** Rental properties have tons of useful deductions. Talk to a CPA to develop a tax strategy that's right for you.

6. **Wealth Creation:** We'd rather be wealthy than rich because it's more sustainable. Also, you're taxed more on income than wealth creation.

We LOVE owning rental properties. We leverage these assets, by getting loans on them. We love the ability to use leverage with banks to buy more properties than we could afford without loans. However, since it's rental property, we're having someone else pay down that loan for us. On top of that we're actually getting a little cash flow too. We love investing in rental properties because of the tax benefits. Also, the value of these properties tends to appreciate (go up in value), assuming we do proper maintenance on them. It's not guaranteed, but rather icing on the cake if that happens. Aside from maintenance, time is the other variable that tends to affect appreciation. The longer you can wait to sell the property, the more likely you could expect some appreciation. Rental properties are great for generating income. We simply charge a higher rent than our expenses. Creating that overage is our cash flow. Then there is wealth creation. We discussed how to achieve wealth creation with all of these factors.

We still love wholesaling too. We are always going to be talking about wholesaling. We like to buy houses directly from the seller because that's how we find the really good deals to turn into rentals; and how we generate extra cash. Wholesaling and BRRRR work so well together.

Action Item: Write down why you'd like to own rental properties. How many? What does freedom mean to you? What does wealth mean to you? Clarity equals power.

*"Wealth is not about having a lot of money,
it's about having a lot of options."*

— Chris Rock

CHAPTER 5

BRRRR Case Study: 2250 Collier Ave.

W e love it when we get a finished product out there. It feels somewhat like a wholesale deal when you close it and get that check. That's fun. It's the same way with rentals. When we finish that project, and start looking for tenants, or shopping for tenants, that's fun. It's just plain fun to have a finished project. The same thing goes with our podcast. We are finally getting some new content out there. It's the same feeling of completion and sharing with everybody the good times. Hopefully you guys like what we're putting out. Check out the podcast at DPIPodcast.com.

This chapter we're talking about a rental property we just finished. This is 2250 Collier, in St Louis, Missouri. Mike managed this project. We bought this property off-market. We rehabbed it and did a rental grade rehab on it. It was never meant to be a flip. We just wanted to rehab it good enough to get a tenant in there and collect rent. Our company bought it as a company purchase.

We don't have tenants in this property yet. However, we've got the security deposit and first month's rent already collected. They're moving in on March 1st. We are still working on refinancing the property though. Just got the appraisal back last night, so all our numbers are basically in. That's pretty exciting, and we will share all that with you.

Our strategy on rentals is to buy, rehab, rent, and refi. We're one step closer to getting the refinance portion done, so we can then take that money and move it to the next project; the repeat part of BRRRR.

This Collier project was a great one. We bought it off market. To give you an idea on the numbers, we paid around $66k. And then we paid someone on our team a little bit for locking it up for us. Since we wanted to buy this one instead of wholesaling it, we paid them a couple of thousand dollars. So, our all-in price to purchase this was $69-70k. We then did the rehab; we had a private lender help us out. So again, we used private funds instead of our own cash or bank money. It's always more fun, and easier to use somebody else's money. It doesn't matter how much money you have. You can still invest in real estate if you find the right deals. Other People's Money (OPM) for the win.

On this rehab, our budget was pretty tight. We'll talk about why, and what we did in just a second. Our rehab budget when we estimated it was about $12k. We expected it to be a relatively easy rehab. $12k is not much at all, looking back in hindsight. By the way, we can only explain so much in a book. We encourage you to watch the video where we walk through the property. Then you'll be able to see the quality of our rehab. You will see the materials we use. You'll see what the finished product looks like, too. Check us out on YouTube or Discount Property Investor Podcast, you'll be able to find this video, It's season 2, episode 2. (We will throw it up on www.FreeLandLordCourse.com in the Case Study section at the end as well) You're definitely going to get a little bit more out of it by watching us walk through and explain things. As we walk through the property, we try to describe everything.

Again, we can only give you so much information out of a book.

We tried to spend $12k. We expected the After Repair Value (ARV) was going to be about $115k when we were done with the project. Our actual numbers came in pretty dang close to that. Looking at the spreadsheet, our actual repair numbers plus holding costs ended up being right at $15k. The holding costs ended up a little higher than we expected, but not much. We expected a little over $12k for the rehab, and around $3k for our holding costs. It's useful to keep these numbers separate for budgeting purposes.

To recap, we bought it for about $70k, and we are into it for a total of $84k. We put just shy of $15k into it. We just got the appraisal back last night and it was a bit lower than we expected. This house is a split-level. The square footage was calculated a bit differently. It was bigger than the surrounding houses in the subdivision. Our guess is that the appraiser clipped us a bit on the appraisal, because this is one of the larger houses in that subdivision. That's fine, we got a $105k appraisal. We were hoping for $115k, but we got $105k. We are into it for $84k. Our re-finance will probably be right around the $84k we're into it. We have several banking partners we are working with, but the banking partner that gives us the best deal at this point in time is 80%. We don't need to pull more money out than that, because we want to have some equity in these properties too. So even if a banking partner said we can do 85-95%, we wouldn't necessarily want to do that. Our goal is twofold; first, to get the passive income from the rental properties, and second, to have some equity build up. We want to pay them off and minimize the risk of overleveraging them. If you are leveraging yourself too high, you are putting that second goal further away. This property is a great example of our BRRRR model. We've got $84,717 into the property, it's appraised at $105k. And the bank will give us $86k, which is 80% of $105k.

We went a couple thousand over budget. That happens. But we should get out exactly what we put into it, the $84k. That's really exciting. We bought it, and it meets our formula perfectly. If we can buy it, rehab it, and get most or all our money back; that is a really exciting project for us. Let's go ahead and jump into the Walk through or onsite video.

*** Walk Through***

*** Visit www.FreeLandLordCourse.com***

Go to the case study section to watch this video

Now that we got the numbers and formula out of the way. Let's take a tour of the rental property itself and describe what renovations we did and our thought process behind our decisions. This 2250 Collier. This is a property we picked up for a pretty good price. We were a little bit tight on our rehab budget. We will show you some of the tricks we used to stay really low on our rehab budget on this one. Let's go ahead and walk inside. It was really cold here in St. Louis this winter, so we didn't do too much to the exterior. But as you walk in, you will see we tried to save the linoleum floor. We are going to keep this for one tenant, possibly two. As you walk through, there was carpet covering up these stairs as well as the flooring. We removed that to expose the hardwood underneath. So, with the flooring we really lucked out. It was in pretty good shape on this one. Instead of having a professional flooring company come through, we just had our general contractor buff the floors, then add a coat of polyurethane. Now we've got wood floors that have been re-finished and look new. That adds value to the home and saves some money for us as well.

The railings were old and black. So, we had them painted white. They now match all the trim in the house, and really pop with freshness. We didn't remove the trim because we didn't have to re-sand the floors, we just coated them as we mentioned earlier.

In the kitchen, we kept the linoleum floors because they were in pretty good shape, we went ahead and saved the linoleum. Again, we'll get through a tenant or two hopefully with this flooring. If it gets beat up, it's not a big deal because we never had to put money into it initially. The cabinets we got from a discount store here in St. Louis. We always shop for sales. So, this is actually two models up from their cheapest level of cabinets. But since they were on sale, it matches their cheapest level. And now we've got solid wood cabinets.

These are from Hoods, a local St Louis hardware store. Another great one is Menard's. We paid $19 for that fridge. It's a used appliance. The ceiling fans we put up in all of our properties are from Lowes. We got the 42-inch ones for most of the rental properties because they're not large spaces. These run around $59, really not that expensive. Not a big offset to our kitchen budget, and they look nice. Traditionally light/fan fixtures are going to be centered more over the eating area whereas this one isn't. We went with track lighting over the kitchen cabinets, so you get more light. Tenants can aim them down when they're cooking. It's a nice feature. All we're missing at the moment is a stove and dishwasher. There is room for a stove and microwave. They're ordered, they just need to be put in. There's no dishwasher. There wasn't one, so we didn't bother replacing it. That's pretty much everything in the kitchen. Again, the fridge, that's my favorite part. We picked that up for $19, killer deal. We didn't even know this until now, but as a lumber yard, they get the old appliances when they go in and pick up other people's appliances. They just threw this one out there for $19. You can't beat that. We are going to go ahead and reset the water filter. Brand new water filter in there for them.

The flooring was in really good shape. As we go into one of the bedrooms, you will see the same ceiling fan we used throughout. We used the stainless finish. And again, we go for the ones that are least expensive and that is a $59 ceiling fan. It looks really nice. We put one of those in each bedroom, and it comes with a great light fixture. We always encourage you to get as many lights as you can on the ceiling fan. We have three LED's, so it's nice and bright in here. This one we saved as much as we could. Again, with this house, we were really tight on the budget. So normally we would replace the doors. On this one though, all the doors were in really good shape, so we just painted them white. It looks nice, and it's clean. Same thing with the bedroom doors themselves. Instead of replacing them, we painted them white, and put new hardware on them. It's going to help us get a decent appraisal out of it, without breaking the bank.

This house is a four-bedroom, two-bath. It's what's called a raised ranch. We have three bedrooms up on the main floor, and one in the basement. The bedrooms are all pretty much the same size. The master bedroom is a bit larger. The only reason we call it the master is because it has two closets, and it has access to the Jack and Jill bathroom. We saved the closet doors in here. They're mirrored, and not in great shape, but we cleaned them up. We still need to get our cleaning crew in here to finish everything. This had a single sink when we bought it, and extra space for them to put stuff. We decided to go ahead and put in a double sink in. It's the only bathroom on the main level, so the Jack and Jill sink make it a bit nicer here. With the flooring, we used a neat trick that Bill, our rental guru uses. It's a peel and stick vinyl tile that is groutable. That means you can literally peel it and stick it down. We leave a little space between tiles that we fill in with grout. It looks just like tile flooring. It holds up better than tile and is a hell of a lot cheaper. Not to mention, any handyman can do this with a limited skill set and tool set.

Let's check out the downstairs. Again, this is our budget buster house, so everything had to be done on the downlow. This house is a raised ranch, or a split level. Those might be a bit different, but that doesn't matter. The bedrooms, kitchen, etc. are up. The main stuff is on the main floor. There is a huge bedroom down here in the basement. It's nice too. It's still got the mini fan. We just painted it and cleaned it up. The carpets were okay. We decided to try and save them for at least one more go around. We had a handyman do the carpet cleaning for us on this one. They're not perfect, but they are pretty clean. It smells good and clean in here, it's great. Same thing over in this living room area. We have one ceiling fan in this area, and then a couple of the dome lights. Those are about $19. This was old wood paneling before. We just painted it the same agreeable grey color that we use throughout the rest of the house. It's a quick fix, because no one likes to look at the old paneling. Now it looks awesome.

We've got the grey walls with the white trim. The whole house looks pretty good. The overall rehab budget on this property was $12k. That's for everything including the kitchen, the bathroom, and all the labor. That's $12k for the whole house, completely rehabbed, and now it looks like an almost brand-new house. That's super low, and that's a great number.

We purchased this home for $70k after we paid our partner for locking up the deal. We had to keep the rehab budget low on this one to get most of the money back out of it. The flooring in the bathroom is the same as upstairs. We went with a cheaper vanity. We use a bit cheaper material in basement bathrooms. Same thing for bathroom lighting; with the basement bathroom, we go for cheaper lighting. This was an exception however; we didn't put a vanity light in because it didn't have one. We didn't need one necessarily because we have a window right behind the door here. It's plenty bright, there's plenty of light coming in. Again, with basement bathrooms, we try to keep them lower budget compared to main floor bathrooms.

On that $12k budget, we didn't even mention that we had a pipe burst. The day we closed on this property; we had a pipe burst. The exterior spigot bust, because it was so cold outside. The seller had turned off the heat. We didn't know about it. We switched over our utilities like we are supposed to, but they turned it off for some reason. What can you do? Just roll with the punches. We came over the same day and turned it back on, however the damage was already done. You can actually see a little bit of difference in paint color. It's definitely handyman quality work, because it's a rental. It's not the finished work we would put in a rehab type project. Since it's a rental, it's no big deal.

On the other side of the basement, we have the utility room. It had a decent furnace. This is what we call a grandma and grandpa house. When you walk into it, everything is well maintained, just not new. It doesn't necessarily look nice. Nothing much back here. We've got the electrician scheduled, and he is going to replace our panel for us. The only thing we had to do was add a new shut off valve to the water line, since we had that pipe burst. We want to prevent that from happening again.

The washer/dryer was left behind by the previous owner. So, we left that for the tenant. We don't provide a washer dryer, so we just left this one where it was. If they don't want it, we will just pick it up. If they want a washer dryer, they've got to bring their own. If that one works, they are welcome to use it.

So that was Collier. That was a quick little walkthrough of the property. Here's a couple of little ending notes. We did go back and put a new filter in the fridge. If you watch the video, some of the work wasn't 100% finished in this video. We did get a stove and microwave in. The electric panel was swapped out. The property is completed now. It's a solid little house. We've got three bedrooms on the upper level and one bath. We've got the jack and Jill vanity in the upstairs bathroom. The master bedroom has access to it, and there's also hall access to that bathroom. Then there is a big basement bedroom which is nice, as well as a bathroom down there. It's a four-bedroom, two full bath property. It's great, a lot of people want that extra space, and be able to move a lot of people in.

The rent on this one will be $1200. Our mortgage with taxes and insurance is going to come out around $800-900. We're still waiting on the final numbers. However, we should be capturing about $3-400 a month in cash flow. This ended up being a pretty good project for us. It was a great case study. It was a success. We purchased the property. Then we rehabbed the property. Now we've got the property rented. Right now, we're still in the process of refinancing the property, but we should be able to get all of our money back. We probably won't cash out any extra money. We're not making money on the deal, but we will get all the money we invested into both the purchase, holding costs, and the rehab back. We're basically into this property for zero money out of pocket. We're into it just for our efforts.

Now we've added an asset to our portfolio. We have a tenant in place that is paying us roughly $400 more a month than what we owe on a debt service; this includes all the expenses, tax and insurance. We do have a management company helping us with this. After we pay the management company maybe we will be bringing in around $350.

It's great, because someone else is paying our mortgage so we're building equity. We're capturing about $350 a month in cash flow, which is definitely taxed a lot lower than regular income. We can depreciate the property to save on our taxes at the end of the year. There are so many advantages to real estate investing, it's crazy. This has been a great case study. Thanks for reading. You definitely want to check out the video. There are going to be more and more of these coming. It's a great case study, but it's also the reason we're not podcasting as much at the moment. We're out there doing deals.

We're glad we could share this side of the business with you. This is what we're teaching some of our other students. Bill, especially, is focused on this side of the business. It's very exciting. This is a bit of a home run for us since the numbers worked out perfect. We've got about ten more case studies/walkthroughs we're going to show you. As time goes on, we'll delve more into the rental side of the business. We'll also show you how to secure private money, how we use it, why we use it, and that sort of stuff. Check out more videos at www.FreeLandlordCourse.com

Part II

THE BUYING PROCESS

CHAPTER 6

The Buying Process

In this section of the book, we're going to cover what to buy, how to buy it, and how to fund it. If you started out wholesaling like us, you should hopefully know your numbers by now. That is a recurring theme with real estate, and with rentals in particular. With rentals, you really have to sharpen that pencil, and know your numbers to a much finer point when you're executing the BRRRR strategy. This is especially true when you're trying to leave as little money (equity) in the property as possible. In this market, the interest rates are low, and prices are slowly climbing here in the Midwest. We definitely want to leverage our money as far as we can. We're trying to leave as little money as possible tied up in the houses so we can continue stretching our money. That is the BRRR Strategy. We Buy, Rehab, Rent, Re-finance, and Repeat. That repeat is what we have to keep harping on.

Step one in this process is finding the deal. Step two is buying and funding it. There's a couple of ways we can use to fund a deal once we know it's one we're keeping.

The Buying Process

We consider ourselves experts at finding deals. That's why we put together a book on it. If you haven't read it yet, our book, "The Ultimate Guide To Wholesaling Real Estate" can be purchased on Amazon. It's a very comprehensive guide to finding the best deals. Even if you're not interested in wholesaling, our information about the buying process is top notch material. To make BRRRR work, you've got to find great deals. That book is full of our best material on finding and negotiating great deals. In that book we cover these topics extensively:

- How To Find the Deal (marketing)
- Following Up
- Setting Up Appointments
- Determining Repairs and Maximum Allowable Offer
- Negotiation

- Getting it under contract

- Finding a title company

- Closing

Rather than re-writing the book on the buying process, we'd prefer you check out that book or go to www.FreeWholesaleCourse.com.

Marketing To Sellers

To find great deals, you need to do your own marketing and get motivated sellers to contact you. Our office motto is, "Keep the best and sell the rest." That's our business model. We wholesale the deals we don't want to keep and keep the best deals we get from our "off market" marketing. That doesn't necessarily mean these properties are a bad deal for someone else. We all have different metrics we use that make sense to our individual business models. The takeaway point is that we know we're getting the properties we want at a significant discount. This is the foundation of the BRRRR strategy. Rule number one, buy at a discount. If you're not buying at a discount, it's very difficult to increase the value of a property enough just from the rehab.

If you read our first book, "The Ultimate Guide to Wholesaling Real Estate", you should have a clear idea of how to find great deals. We cover the buying process extensively in that book. We assume that by reading this book, you are starting a business and plan to invest in Real Estate for the long run. Real estate is not a get rich quick scheme, but rather a build wealth slow game.

We want to not only accumulate rentals but build a profitable wholesale business as well. Think of rentals as your day to day paycheck. They will be there for you, and you can count on them as regular paychecks. Think of your wholesale pipeline as a feeder for rentals or for rehab flips or wholesale flips. These are a bonus on top of your rental income.

Now that you understand where we are coming from, we can give you the following advice. We want you to build a marketing pipeline because going direct to the seller is the best way to find deals on properties. This can be a big investment of time or money, but it needs to be done consistently. While you are just getting started it's good to establish relationships with real estate agents and other wholesalers. We recommend going to networking and real estate specific networking events. You can learn what other local investors are doing and get tips and assistance from them. The more you're helping others in your area, the more you tend to get in return.

Making Offers

An easy way to find deals quickly for a rental investor or rehabber is the start working with wholesalers. A wholesaler's entire job is to find good deals to sell to rental investors or rehabbers. However, just because someone is a wholesaler or selling a property off market does not make it a good deal automatically. You need to do your research and determine if it is. We'll discuss the MAO formula in the next chapter. That is what you will use to determine if you have a good deal. MAO stands for "maximum allowable offer" and is determined by taking the "after repair value" multiplied by the discount rate and subtracting repairs. We generally get houses at about 50%-60% of their ARV. If houses in an area are selling for $100,000, we usually want to buy it around $50,000 to $60,000 if it needs some work.

Don't be afraid to make those low offers. The property may be listed for $70,000 or $80,000, but you never know what the seller needs to get for it. One of our favorite sayings is, "Writing a contract and submitting an offer is just the beginning of the conversation." If you are working with an agent or negotiating directly with the seller, that contract is still just the beginning of the conversation. So get out there and make a ton of offers. It is the only way you are going to get a property under contract. That's the only way you're going to buy a house in the United States, especially at a discount.

> *"Writing a contract and submitting an offer is just the beginning of the conversation."*

Inspections

When you get a property under contract, this is when the inspection period starts. Now you have the opportunity to have the house inspected. How you decide to do that is entirely up to you. In residential sales most people have a professional home inspector look at the property. The professional home inspector will prepare an inspection report that can be between 20 and 150 pages. It will contain multiple things that the home inspector will recommend repairing. You do not have to get a home inspection to be in this business. Typically, we order a sewer lateral camera inspection and that's it. The sewer lateral inspection is important to us because it's one of the only areas we cannot see when walking through, and sewer lateral problems can be costly to repair.

We recommend new investors to get a sewer lateral and a bid from at least one contractor during the inspection. This way you will have a bid to do the repairs that you believe will need to be done. Now that you have a property under contract and have a bid from a contractor or the results of the sewer lateral, you can either continue with the purchase or go back to the seller and tell them you found some other issues. Now is your chance to renegotiate the price or exercise your right to walk away from the contract by signing a mutual release. We almost always try to renegotiate the price in these situations.

Closing

Once you are under contract with the property, you'll need to bring the purchase contract and earnest deposit money to a title company or closing attorney if you are not working with an agent. This is typically something a real estate agent would do for you. Title companies are fairly easy to find. We recommend asking some of those people you network with locally who they use and find out if they are investor friendly. I would not recommend asking for a discount right away but if you bring a lot of business to the same company, they may have some flexibility in their price for you.

There are a ton of ways to fund deals too, even if you don't have the cash. We'll discuss your options in a later chapter. Finding a way to fund a deal is really the only difference in the buying process compared to finding a deal to wholesale. The exit strategy involves finding funding instead of an end buyer.

Recap:

1. **The Buying Process:** We cover this extensively in "The Ultimate Guide To Wholesaling." Getting a good deal is crucial for any real estate niche, especially wholesaling and rentals using the BRRRR strategy.

2. **Marketing To Sellers:** The best way to find deals is to deal directly with the seller.

3. **Making Offers:** Real estate is a numbers game. You need to make a ton of offers to get the best deals. Making an offer is just the start of the conversation.

4. **Inspections:** We typically get sewer lateral inspections because we can't visually see what's going on in the sewer lateral, and these tend to be costly repairs. The inspection period allows for renegotiating too.

5. **Closing:** Title companies or a closing attorney are where you'd take a signed contract to be executed. There are a ton of ways to fund deals to close on them.

Pick the area that works best for you. Then use our model of keeping the best properties that fit your buying criteria and sell the rest. Wholesale them off, keep the best ones. For us, keeping the best means we're buying a property that fits into the BRRRR strategy. That means we buy a property, start fixing it up, get an occupancy inspection, get it rented, then take it to a bank to do a refinance on it. It's a process. We want properties that make this transition as smooth as possible.

Action Item: Review our book, "The Ultimate Guide To Wholesaling." Or check out our online course, www.FreeWholesaleCourse.com. Even if you're more interested in renting property than wholesaling, you still have to buy properties at a discount. Our book and course teach you how.

"If I had six hours to chop down a tree, I'd spend the first four sharpening the axe." -Abraham Lincoln

CHAPTER 7

Defining Buying Criteria

What to Purchase

Typically, we're looking for houses with three or more bedrooms and at least one and a half bathrooms. These are the best houses for us.

If we come across a house with less bedrooms, our exit strategy is generally to wholesale or wholetail them. We're not interested in buying those houses, because in our experience, they typically don't work for us. We have parameters set for what we're looking for. For example, it's hard to charge enough rent to cover the mortgage with most one-bedroom units. Whenever you end up buying a house, and rehabbing it, it costs money. Granted, with the BRRRR strategy, you'll be able to get all that money back when you refinance. However, you're going to have a very high mortgage after you buy, rehab, and refinance.

We like single family homes. Single family homes are traditionally one of the best things to invest in. The US has seen about a 6% value increase annually (appreciation) from the 1960's prior to the bust and then back through the recovery. Rental income is stabilizing again and that's adjusted for inflation.

Avoid One Bedroom Homes

Construction quality affects your construction costs. A one-bedroom home still has one kitchen and one bathroom. It still has one roof too and all of the components like electric, plumbing, water, HVAC, etc. You still have to repair all those things, but you only have one bedroom to collect rent from. Not to mention, the bedroom is the cheapest part in the whole scheme of your rehab construction. Fixing up another bedroom is very inexpensive. It's inexpensive to replace flooring, doors, paint, or fix a light fixture compared to replacing plumbing, electric, cabinets, etc. While it is cheap to rehab a bedroom, it's expensive to add an addition on to a house. If those other bedrooms aren't already built into the house, it's not always feasible to add them on.

The cost of rehabbing a one bedroom is relatively the same as a house with more bedrooms, but you're not going to get as much for rent. There's less demand for one-bedroom houses. So that's why we, and a lot of other investors stick to three bedrooms or more. At the end of the day, a deal is a deal though. The numbers have to make sense. We also like to look for opportunities to add bedrooms. By this we mean convert a large bedroom into two bedrooms or convert an extra dining room or living room into an additional bedroom. This can be done relatively inexpensively and is much more feasible than creating an addition. Typically adding a wall, door, and a closet will give you another bedroom if the space allows.

Multi-Family Homes Vs. Single Family Homes

There is a big difference between a single-family rental and a multi-family rental. With a multi-family, you get to spread your repair/maintenance costs over multiple units. For example, if you own a multi-family property, you might have one roof with ten individual one-bedroom units. It changes the way the math is done for getting accurate numbers. The type of property has a lot to do with what kind of investing or investor you want to become or do.

If you're just getting started, we recommend sticking to single families. They are easy to manage, and they are easier to work the numbers on if you're a beginner. Figure out what kind of investing you want to do and stick to it.

There are pros and cons of multi-families versus single families. When we say multi-family, we're talking about 4 or more units, not duplexes. First, the barriers to entry are going to be higher typically when you have a multi-family. Since they're larger buildings, by their nature, you're going to have a lot more plumbing, more electrical work, etc. The total repair costs are going to be higher. Our second biggest issue of multi-family properties is they lack liquidity. By comparison, single family houses are very easy to sell because there are a lot of buyers out there looking for single family homes. Not only are there more investors looking to buy single family homes, but there are also a lot of people wanting to buy a house just to move into. With multi-family investments, the owner typically doesn't live in them. This means you're always going to be dealing with an investor whenever you buy or sell larger properties. It's also easier to get a bank loan on single family homes. Banks aren't as comfortable taking on that risk until you've built up your experience level with a proven track record.

Knowing what you're looking for in advance is going to help you out tremendously. Are you buying a single family? Are you trying to buy a multi-family? It's not advisable to just go out and start shopping without knowing what you're trying to buy.

Location

Location, location, location. It's so important. As you know, we live in and do business in St. Louis. We have rentals in the south city and north county regions primarily. Although we have some rentals sprinkled out in other areas too.

Before buying a property, it's important to educate yourself. Find and attend a REIA (Real Estate Investment Association). You can network and find out where other people are investing.

When purchasing rentals, it is very important to know your numbers, but also the location. The location of the property is going to greatly affect those spreads and those numbers. Certain parts of town have what we call class A properties, or class B, class C, or even class D properties. For clarification, you can sometimes buy a property in one area for half the cost of a similar sized house in another area. So, the location is very, very important.

We give them a scale of A, B, C, and D to describe them. Some areas are prone to negative cash flow. This means the amount of money it costs to buy and fix up a property is more than we can collect in rent. We want to find areas that provide high cash flow but are inexpensive. We're looking for a sweet spot. Class A properties are nice and desirable neighborhoods; however, these houses are generally owned by owner-occupants. They don't cash flow as well as what we'd describe as B and C areas.

People might define these asset classes differently. But we define B and C areas, as desirable areas. The people who live there are generally working class and people want to live in these areas. It's a good mix of homeowners and landlords. The property values tend to stay up because the landlords and other owners tend to maintain their properties in these areas.

The definitions of Class A, B, C, D are not very uniform when talking to different investors. Some only use ABC to define classes. We designate four classes because it helps us wrap our mind around the quality of the neighborhood. We tend to look at this as a sliding scale. Below is how we generally define or identify the classes.

Class A: These houses are generally in the most desirable areas of the city. They have the top-rated school districts, well maintained neighborhoods, and a high percent of owner occupants as opposed to tenant occupied properties. There's often new construction within the past 15 years or so.

Class B and C: We tend to lump these together but consider it a sliding scale. These areas will be solid working-class areas. Crime is relatively low in these areas. You should still feel comfortable walking around these areas day or night. There's a mix of owner-occupied housing and tenant occupied properties. Class B are higher end neighborhoods compared to Class C. However, these shift along the scale. There are no hard rules, but rather guidelines. If landlords or tenants are not maintaining their properties high standards, you might be more on the Class C side than Class B. However, the numbers should still work; and banks are generally happy to lend in these areas.

Class D: These are areas we try to avoid buying in. These are commonly referred to as "war zones". We definitely have some of those in St. Louis. If you have ever seen the original National Lampoon's Vacation movie, there's an iconic scene where "Clark is lost in the hood". While he stops to ask for directions, the wheels are taken off his car. That scene is a funny caricature of the rough neighborhoods in St. Louis. However, crime is usually higher in Class D neighborhoods.

Almost all of the properties are tenant occupied, vacant, or boarded up. This is not an area you would feel comfortable visiting, day or night. We tend to avoid buying in Class D areas.

"There's so much less research involved when investing in the same area than trying to go somewhere we don't know anything about."

In short, Class A areas are too expensive to provide a decent return on investment (ROI). Class D areas are in such disrepair or are in such little demand that they don't provide a decent return on investment either. Class B and C are the sweet spots, and just refer to which end of the spectrum we're on.

If you live in an affluent neighborhood for example, you might be driving by million dollar houses each day. It doesn't necessarily make sense to buy something close to you just because you live in an area and you are comfortable with it. You may have to get out of your comfort zone and invest in an area that makes sense from a numbers perspective. You really need to know your numbers, so you can make better cash flow.

In St. Louis, we tend to invest in the north county and the south city areas. Occasionally we can find some west county where the numbers make sense. We suggest starting by looking in your local area, because you're going to be more familiar with it hopefully. But that doesn't necessarily mean that's where the best deals are. You don't necessarily need to invest in your backyard, but you should be smart with your money.

Why does that location matter for us? It's simple. We invest in those two particular areas of St Louis because the numbers work. We know we can generate positive cash flow in those areas. It's proven because we are doing it.

Let's compare an expensive market to a less expensive market. For example, the west coast, especially California, have crazy expensive real estate in our opinion compared to what we can buy in the Midwest. A two-bedroom, one bath bungalow might cost $500,000 in high density areas in California. That type of property wouldn't make sense for us to buy as a rental in most cases, at least not where we live here. Not to mention, it's harder to come up with money for a $500,000 house than a $100,000 house. The rent certainly isn't going to be five times as high, so it doesn't make sense from a ROI standpoint.

Getting back to the Midwest, you should look for areas that make sense to invest in from a cash flow perspective. You need to look at the purchase price, figure out what you can finance the properties for, break down what your monthly payments are going to be, figure out your taxes and insurance costs on it, and your estimated rents.

Local Laws

We suggest you get really familiar with your city and county rental laws. There are particular areas in St. Louis that will charge a fee for you to own a rental property or require you to have a license. There are some municipalities that regulate the percentage of rentals in a particular neighborhood, by street, or even within condo complexes. If that house wasn't already a rental you won't be able to rent that house if that neighborhood has reached a rental quota. You definitely want to be familiar with the local laws before you jump in and spend time and money buying a property that you might not even be able to rent out.

In St Louis, specifically St Louis county, we have many other municipalities within it. These municipalities have their own jurisdiction and unique laws. For example, if you own property in unincorporated St. Louis county, you deal with St. Louis county inspectors. However, if you're in a municipality that is incorporated such as Berkley, then you'd have to deal with Berkley's inspectors. Berkley in particular has a law that states you can only have a certain number of rentals on a particular street. The reason a law like this might get passed is it's a great idea to keep up property values. Tenants quite often don't keep up with maintenance as much as a homeowner. Too many tenants in one area has a tendency to drive down property prices. That may have been the case when Berkley implemented this idea 50 years ago. However, Berkley is and already has been a rental area. It's kind of unfortunate. The area has already turned kind of slummy, and this law discourages investors from buying property in that area. Investor money could be what's needed to invigorate that part of town. It's a catch 22.

They put this rule into place because a majority of the area were already rentals. There's an assumption that investors don't care for the properties as well as owner occupants. It's assumed that primary residents are more willing to invest into a home that they live in. The problem with that is, there are not enough people in that area that can or are willing to invest money into a property. In this case, investors are really the only option. So that's the catch from the way we see it. The people implementing the law might have had sound logic and good intentions, but we believe it's making the situation worse.

Other Factors and Considerations

Another issue that can affect property values is how banks lend money. In Berkley, some houses are worth around $60,000 on the high end. However, most of them are probably only $20-30,000 properties realistically. Not many banks are willing to lend on $20-30,000 properties. If people can't get a loan from a bank, then the only people that can buy houses in that area are cash buyers. These are just a couple of examples of what might affect property values in an area. So it's really important to not only be familiar with a given area, but also the laws, and other factors that might have an impact on property values, unforeseen costs, and rentability of a given property. Flood zones are another thing to watch out for, because this could affect insurance prices. Some areas have higher property taxes than others too.

Recap:

1. **What to Purchase:** We purchase single family homes with 3 or more bedrooms. They're easy to rent, easy to repair, and get the best ROI.

2. **Avoid One Bedroom Homes:** These are hard to rent, and repair costs are high compared to how much they can be rented for.

3. **Multi-Family Homes Vs. Single Family Homes:** Multi-family homes come with some advantages; however, we don't recommend them for new investors.

Repairs are expensive, the numbers are trickier, and it's harder to get funding or sell them if need be.

4. **Location:** We break areas down into Class A, B, C, and D. This is a spectrum, and the goal is to land in the sweet spot of B and C.

5. **Local Laws:** Local laws can vary between municipalities and might not be obvious at first glance. Take the time to learn these laws, because they can affect inspections and rentability.

6. **Other Factors and Considerations:** Keep your eye open for other factors that might affect rentability or your ROI.

Action Item: Get familiar with the differences between Class A-D properties. Can you tell the difference when you drive around? Can you circle and label them on a map? Knowing where you're going to buy is extremely before you start shopping around.

"Success occurs when opportunity meets preparation." -Zig Ziglar

CHAPTER 8

Property Analysis

Construction Quality

We just discussed what kind of houses you should buy, and how to evaluate areas to buy in. This chapter is about how to evaluate a house once you find one that fits your buying criteria. Once we determine the condition, we're going to put a plan in place to get that property fixed up and ready to be rented out. We'll go into depth about project planning more when we talk about rehabbing in a later chapter. We'll discuss different ways to estimate repairs and figure out what your rehab costs are going to be. However, this chapter is meant to be an overview of the process.

Bed/bath count is very important, but so is construction quality. Things to factor in are if the house has a basement, a garage, a yard, etc. These things are going to be very different from market to market. However, these qualities can affect rentability if something that's typical in an area is missing or substandard. In St Louis, where we invest, 95% of the houses have basements. However, we're aware that some cities have no basements at all, or just a crawl space is common. So, it really matters to understand what's normal/abnormal to your market if you're going to buy something to rent out.

That extra storage/living space of a garage or basement could be really important to your possible tenants. You want to be able to provide your tenant(s) with all the possible things they may need. Remember, they're your customers, if storage is something important to them, you need to be able to provide it. Basements are also used for safety purposes in the Midwest because tornadoes can be somewhat common. They're also common in St. Louis because our soil allows for it. We're generally not dealing with bedrock or an elevated water table like other parts of the country. Although basements don't count towards square footage according to the tax records, they certainly can add extra living space or storage space. Basements are awesome. If basements are common in your area, it's also important to watch out for signs of water damage to leaky basement, or sewer backups.

Garages also allow for extra storage, especially for things you can't or don't want to keep in the house. They can also be used as a parking spot for your tenant's vehicles. A lot of people don't want to leave their car out on the street, because the sun is going to tear up the paint and deteriorate the car as well. Hail, snow, or even the possibility of being broken into make garages more attractive to prospective tenants. So being able to offer somebody covered parking or even the secured parking a garage can provide, is definitely going to increase the value of the home. This allows you to charge even more for rent since it's an added value. A yard might be a selling point for a renter with kids, a dog, or just a place to have a BBQ with friends.

Condition and Repairs

The condition is going to vary greatly from property to property. If the condition is move-in ready, then it doesn't play a big part of the equation. However, if the property needs

$10k to $30k worth of work in order to get an occupancy permit or make it livable we'll have to decrease our offer price accordingly. We operate in St. Louis and most of our local municipalities require occupancy permits. That may not be the case where you are located. Most of the properties we buy are in some form of disrepair. That's how we get them at a discount.

That's the beautiful thing about wholesaling too. The formula is basically the same. If you've followed along with us, then you should've started learning how to calculate your numbers by wholesaling properties. Hopefully you've been going out and making offers on properties. If you've gotten some under contract and marketed to other investors, then you should've gotten some real-world feedback. Other investors might say your rehab number is too low. They might say, "You think I can rehab a 2,000 square foot house that needs a new kitchen, three new bathrooms for $20,000? You're crazy." Or maybe you were spot on and sold a couple deals. Either way, the only way you're going to learn your market is by making offers, and we suggest start getting experience by wholesaling.

Condition is going to be variable from property to property, even with houses in the same neighborhoods built at the same time. We highly encourage you to network with other investors and do some wholesaling to learn how to buy and sell properties. You really need to find out what a good deal looks like in your area to get started. That's where we both got started. We knew we wanted to own rentals, but we started with wholesaling here in St Louis. We grew and started picking up quite a few more. It gets to be really fun.

The rehab estimate is what we're looking for whenever we talk about the condition. How much is it going to cost to fix the property up? Once we know the repair cost, it's pretty easy to use the formula and determine how much we'd be willing to purchase the property for. We use the equation to determine what that purchase price is every single time. It takes the guesswork out. We have a couple of ways to estimate the cost of rehab. Even if you've never done a rehab or wholesaled a deal, you can use these methods to help you determine the rehab cost.

The first rule is the 'Rule of 5s'. We make an estimate of the rehab cost by assigning $5,000 to each "item" that needs rehab. If it needs a bathroom, a roof, an HVAC system, windows, paint and lighting, or flooring we add $5K to the rehab budget for each of those items. A new kitchen or roof might be $10K, but it's still a multiple of 5. For example, if a house needs paint and lighting ($5K), flooring ($5K), a new kitchen ($10k), and a new bathroom ($5k). That house could need $25k in repairs. We've also started to add a misc. $5K because we seem to always find things. Having a little padding helps keep us under budget. This is something quick and simple that works for the Midwest. However, more expensive markets like on the coasts, can have different numbers. You may have to adjust it to the 'Rule of 10s' if this is the case.

The second way we determine repair costs is using a square foot multiplier. This method is useful because it's based on costs in your area and the quality of the rehab. It's very simple for a quick estimate. If it's a light rehab, we might assign it $10/sq. ft, a medium rehab would be $20/sq. ft, and a gut rehab could cost $30-40/sq. ft. Then choose that number and multiply it by the square foot of the house. If it's a 1,000 sq. ft house and just needs light fix up paint and cleaning and some lights you can multiply 1000sqft x $10/sq. ft, and figure on $10K for the rehab. If the house needs more work, bump up the price per sq. ft accordingly.

The third way, and most accurate, is to get bids. This is really only for properties you already have under contract. You can call a general contractor or two and have them give you an estimate. You can walk through the house with them and tell them everything you think needs to be fixed. You should also ask them for what they think needs to be repaired. Stay away from letting them know it's a "rental rehab". General contractors will often skimp on the rehab if they think it's just for a rental property. However, that doesn't fit with the BRRRR model. You really need to improve the property, not just "put lipstick on it". It will hold its value longer, appraise higher, and rent easier if you don't skimp on the rehab. Also, you don't want to drag a bunch of contractors out if you're not actually buying it or intending to use them. Please be courteous when asking others to come give you free estimates.

Rent Amount

The rent amount is a number that affects the viability of a potential rental property. You need an accurate rent estimate for your property to determine if it is going to cash flow for you. We use the 1% rule. This means that your rent should collect at least 1% of the ARV (or appraised value). You should get at least $1000 on a property worth $100k. We often try to go for a bit more. It can be a bit aggressive to go after 2%. That would be trying to collect $1000 on a property that is $50K. The challenge with going for a high rent on a lower value property tends to lead to higher turnover. The tenants also seem to be a little harder on properties in those cases too.

You can find rent estimates in several places online: Zillow.com, rent-o-meter, (https://bit.ly/RentOmeter), or rent.com. They pull rent data from other postings on to their website. They come up with a pretty decent average rent for an area. It works great for tenants too. These websites help give the tenants an idea of what properties are renting for in a given area. It's easy to search the municipality or zip code to see what's available. You can compare the quality of your rental to other properties in the area, to know if you're offering a competitive rate. All the pieces and numbers tie together. A well rehabbed and updated property can command slightly higher rent than an outdated or ugly looking house. When you look at rent estimates, it's important to factor in the quality of your rehab into what you expect to collect in rent.

Expected Cash Flow

It's best to have a property where the tenant(s) can pay you at least $300 more than your PITI (Principal, Interest, Taxes, Insurance). It can be very difficult to rent out a one bedroom for $800-900 bucks in St. Louis, unless you do a really nice job on it, and it's in a really nice area. However, this usually results in a more expensive property and may not fit the 1% rule. We recommend you target cash flow at $300/monthor more. This is after all of your expenses on the property. We use a simple spreadsheet to calculate our numbers, so we can quickly analyze a property. We recommend you set up a similar spreadsheet to analyze your metrics too. You can find the sheet we use at www.FreeLandlordCourse.com and downloading the rental analyzer.

There are things you can control and things you cannot control. Taxes are one of the things you cannot control but should be aware of. Make sure you know what your monthly taxes are for a property. Even though it is possible to renegotiate taxes through the board of appeals, we never assume we'll get a better deal. They are what they are and, in all likelihood, will increase.

Insurance is another huge expense. We've stopped shopping around for a little while. We are happy with our current carrier. We use Lloyds of London / SES. When you're just starting out, we recommend that you call your current insurance agent for your principal residence. If you don't have a principal residence that you own, then call the person that does your auto insurance. When you bundle your insurance, you'll often get lower rates. You can also use google to find homeowner insurance. You can get multiple quotes. Just make sure you get a policy declaration sheet, so you know that you're comparing similar coverage. It's extremely important to consider deductible amounts when shopping for insurance. We like to get coverage with a higher deductible because we don't plan on submitting small claims. This lowers our monthly premium significantly.

Other expenses that affect cash flow are the utilities, and who pays for them. If you purchase a single-family home, it's a good idea to pay the trash service in your name, and then bill it back to the tenant. We do this so that we know a tenant has trash service. We don't want tenants cutting costs and leaving a mountain of trash behind in the property. In St. Louis, our sewer company will attach a lien to the property if the bill is not paid, because you can't exactly turn off the sewer like water or electricity. The sewer bill is attached to the owner, not the user. We like to bill the tenant back for this as well. We also bill the tenants back by having a fixed amount they pay each month added to the lease. We try to cover those costs without making it a profit center. We require the tenants to put other utilities in their name. The other utility companies (gas, electric, cable, etc.) attempt to collect from the tenant not the owner of the property if money is due.

Finally, the last expense is factoring in vacancies, maintenance, and property management into our equation. If you're managing the property yourself, you might not need to factor in property management as an expense. However, there will always be maintenance and vacancies. If you factor these to be around 12% of your gross income, it should cover these expenses

The cash flow is the money that's left over after all of your expenses. We typically look for properties that can at least cash flow $300/month. This typically translates around 30% of the monthly rent that should be cash flow.

We like to Target properties with rent around $1,000 a month. At $1,000 a month, we find a slightly higher caliber tenant. This number may vary in your area. When we have a rental property that has $1,000/month rent, we typically find that the tenants have decent jobs and the ability to pay rent on time. They tend to take care of our property better too. When we start dipping into $700/month to $800/month or less, we find we have higher turnover costs and maintenance expenses. We tend to go for b-class properties because of this. There's a fine line between a higher return on paper and an actual higher return in real life.

To make this a profitable business, and not just a hobby, we need at least $250/month otherwise we risk losing money on the deal. Ideally, we'll have enough cash flow to save some extra money to cover the mortgage when your property is vacant or has big repairs.

Price Point

Price is clearly one of the most important factors when buying a house. Typically, in our area we need rent to be at least 1% of the purchase price plus repairs. This means that if we're looking at a property and think we can get around $900 a month in rent for it. Then the absolute most we can be into this property for is 90K. Your market may be a little different, but it's a great rule of thumb called the 1% rule.

Only three things matter in real estate, the price, the location, and the condition. Once you buy, you can't change the location. It is something that you want to be very intentional. And really, how much you buy a property for is going to play a huge factor in what repairs you can do to affect the condition and/or sell the property later for profit. That's why it's so crucial to buy right. You pick the property, then you get to negotiate the price. The price is going to be based on the rental income in that area. You're going to have to make a judgement call if a purchase at a given price makes sense in that area. Is the purchase price supported by the expected rent? Is there a demand for renters in that area?

You will also use comps (comparable properties) in the area to help you determine the right price. If you are not a licensed agent or have one that is willing to provide you with comps, you'll have to find another way to get good comps when buying an off-market property. You will need access to reliable comps. You can visit http://dpipodcast.com/comps/ to pull comps from the same provider that we use.

Maximum Allowable Offer

Location and type of property are important. However, condition makes a big difference too, especially in regard to rent. We need to make sure our property cash flows properly. Knowing what we can charge for rent, and what repairs are needed are factors in deciding how much we're willing to pay for the property. We need to know that we're still going to be making money after we pay our bills.

The condition is going to affect a lot of things when it comes to how much you can offer on a property. Whenever we look at the property, we start with the end number in mind for the purchase price. We use a simple formula called the MAO (Maximum Allowable Offer) formula. The formula takes the guesswork out of what we can offer for a given property. It's based on what we think the property is going to be worth once it is fixed up to rent quality. We'll cover this in depth in later chapters.

For now, what you need to know is that repairs are basically the thing that is going to change the most in your calculations. If we're going to look at every house on a street and they are all three-bedroom houses, we can assume they have roughly the same after repair value of all these houses. For example, we were analyzing a property this morning, and we looked at a different one on the same street a couple of weeks prior. We figured this house would be pretty similar to the other one. We were right. In fact, the entire street was full of two beds, one bath houses. They were all about 900 to 1000 square feet. We knew the ARV (After Repair Value) was going to be the same, but the condition could vary a lot. The discount rate would be the same because of the location. But the condition is the one thing that varies from house to house.

We use a formula called MAO (Maximum Allowable Offer) for determining our offer price. It's in large part based on the condition. ARV is what you think the house will be worth once it's fixed up. The discount factor is a part of the formula that ensures we're getting a good deal on the property. It's usually a range to where we only pay 70%-80% of the value of the home, depending on the area. To determine which discount factor we use, we base it on the area or the class of the property. A nicer property is going to have a discount factor of around 80%. Whereas a Class C property would be a discount rate at 70% which means you need to get a bigger discount on the property, 30% off.

We multiply the ARV by .7 or .8. Then we subtract the repairs to get our MAO

ARV x (discount factor) - repairs = MAO

(.7 to .8)

ROI Analysis

We like the 1% rule. It's simple and easy. We like to analyze our properties via the cash flow of a property. Since our goal is to pull all the equity out of a property, we won't have much invested in the properties. Therefore, Return on Investment (ROI), doesn't matter to us in the same way as it does for other investors. Other people sometimes make calculations a different way. A common phrase is "cash on cash return". This can be a great way to analyze an investment. The cash on cash return goes up with leverage. It's beautiful. Leverage is tied to the cash on cash return. If we invest $100 into an asset and sell it a year later for $200 with no loan, we made a 100% cash on cash return. However, if we only invest $20, and get a loan for $80 to buy that $100 asset, then we leveraged our money. We'd be buying that asset similar to the way we get a loan on a house. So now we'd have an asset worth $100, but we only paid $20 for. If we sell it for $200 like the example above, then we're only in it for $20. We'd pay back that $80 that was loaned to us, and we'd now have $120. We turned $20 into

$120, that's a 6-fold increase. That's a 600% cash on cash return on our investment. That's the power of leverage.

Another way to look at the cash on cash return is dividing your rental income by the amount invested. For example, if we bought a property by

"We like the 1% rule. It's simple and easy. We like to analyze our properties via the cash flow of a property."

putting $20,000 of our money down, then we could look at how much we're making in rent annually on that property. If we are making $5000 annually from that property, then that would be $5000 income for that $20,000 invested. That would be a 25% cash on cash return.

There are different ways to look at it. That's the cash on cash return method. A lot of people use cap rates (capitalization rates) too. Cap rates are used a lot when comparing multifamily or commercial properties. We're not big fans of using cap rates to analyze properties. We don't like them. But a lot of people use them, especially the big boys. We're just small fish. If you're dealing with a lot of money, you're just looking for just a simple ratio. Cap rate is short for capitalization rate. It's commonly used in real estate and refers to the rate of return on a property based on the net operating income (NOI) that property generates. In other words, a capitalization rate is a return metric that is used to determine the potential return on investment or payback of capital. That's what a cap rate is. The cap rate is determined by taking the net operating income divided by the current market value of the asset. It's kind of silly to us. We hear people saying, "This property has a 14 cap, that one is an 18 cap."

Some of these big firms will buy out at a six or an eight cap. These are low percentages in our mind. They care about different things and have different goals though. They're not looking for as high of a return as us. Our goal is cash flow and wealth creation. Their goal is wealth conservation or preservation, as opposed to creation. When looking to invest in assets and maintain them, those lower cap rates are steadier, and more stable investments. They make sense for them. For us, we're trying to create wealth, so we focus on cash flow. It makes more sense for people starting out. We're small fish in the grand scheme of things. Cash flow is easy. We described cap rates just so you know it's out there. However, we suggest you focus on the cash flow of that asset day one.

Recap:

1. **Construction Quality:** There are things that are not feasible to change with a house once it's bought. A garage and basement can be very useful storage areas for the tenant. Make sure your house is typical for your area.

2. **Condition and Repairs:** This is going to be the variable that changes the most when figuring out your offer price. We use the rule of 5's and the sq. ft. method to determine repair costs.

3. **Rent Amount:** You can use websites like rentometer.com and zillow.com to determine what you should charge for rent. We like using the 1% rule.

4. **Expected Cash Flow:** We like to make at least $250-300/month to make sure we'll profit over the long run.

5. **Price Point:** You can't change many factors once you buy, so it's best to go into buying with a plan. Comps are very helpful.

6. **Maximum Allowable Offer:** We need to buy at a discount to make the BRRRR strategy work. Using this formula takes the guesswork out of making an offer.

7. **ROI Analysis:** There are many ways people calculate their return on investments like cash on cash return or cap rates. We prefer the 1% rule because it's easy.

Action Item: Get comfortable using these formulas. As you walk through a house, use the rule of 5's and the sq. ft. method. How do they compare? Do you like one better than the other? Go on Zillow or Rentometer and compare sale prices to rent amounts. Are there parts of your city that are closer to 1% than others?

"We are what we repeatedly do. Excellence, then, is not an act, but a habit." -Aristotle

CHAPTER 9

Funding the Purchase

Not everyone has a giant pile of cash sitting around or a bunch of private lenders waiting to give them money. Don't stress though if that's the way you feel. There are a bunch of ways to fund the purchase of a property. We're drawing from real world experience and can give you plenty of options depending on your situation.

It's important to outgrow the fear based, scarcity mindset. You need to have an abundance mindset when you're in this business and with life in general. There are plenty of deals out there for those willing to find them. There's lots of ways to fund purchase. There's cash, bank loans, private money or hard money, and creating your own funds.

When you start looking for properties to buy, you need to have metrics in place for the type of property, so you can determine your cash flow before you even buy the property. Especially if you have funding in place with one of the several options we mentioned; cash, bank loan, private money loan, hard money loan, or the more advanced strategy of creating a fund.

Cash

The first option would be cash. If you have a bunch of cash you need to invest, rentals are a great way to get a high return on your investment. You could go out and buy a property for cash and leave all your money in it. We typically receive about a thousand bucks a month rent for a $100k property. That's around a 12% return on your investment.

As a wholesaler, you're usually telling the seller that you're a cash buyer who can close quickly. And that's true because when you buy at a steep enough discount, finding cash is easy. It's easy to find a cash buyer to partner with to buy that deal.

Cash has the least number of obstacles. You don't have to deal with a lender slowing things down. You don't have to get an appraisal upfront. If you're new to this, you might be thinking you don't have much access to cash. If that's the way you feel, we recommend going back to our free wholesale course at www.FreeWholesaleaCourse.com. After you do some wholesaling, you can start to stockpile some cash. You might be able to stockpile enough cash to buy your first rental. Rentals aren't always $100,000 properties. We buy tons of houses that are $15,000 to $30,000 and they make decent rentals. Sometimes we get properties as low as $5-10,000. It really just depends on your buying criteria and finding deals that make sense for where you're at in your real estate investing career.

Cash is definitely the easiest way to fund your purchase. It's quick, less difficult, and has less fees too. At the end of the day, it's also cheaper to use cash. When you borrow money, you'll have to pay interest on the money you borrow. The only cost associated with cash is the opportunity costs of spending the money on this property...until you refinance.

Private Funding

The next easiest way to fund a purchase would be using private money. We're calling this type of funding a "one to one". This means that when somebody has money to lend to you to buy a house, they put a lien on that property. They have secured their investment with that real estate. You (the borrower) own it, and you pay them back with principal and interest. The individual that loaned that money is acting in place of a bank. Whatever payment plans you work out with that individual is between you and them. That's why it's called a private loan. You find it and work on it, and they fund it. Everybody wins.

Private lending doing one offs like this is a little bit easier to do than pooling funds from multiple people. Pooling funds can be pretty tricky. You don't

"Finding private lenders might be easier than you think. Anyone you know might be a potential private money lender."

really want to do that unless you know what you're doing. We'll discuss that strategy later in this chapter. It's much better to find one lender to fund one deal for you. You can purchase that one property and rehab it.

Finding private lenders might be easier than you think. Anyone you know might be a potential private money lender. If you know someone with money, you can just ask them to borrow it. It could be your mom, dad, aunt, uncle, rich cousin, grandparents, or friends. A lot of people have retirement accounts, sometimes with hundreds of thousands of dollars in those accounts. They could be making anywhere from 2-6% on that money. That's a slow way to grow your money, when you can offer them 8-14% to borrow that money. Not to mention, that money is secured by the hard asset of real estate. That doesn't mean it's 100% risk averse. However, Real Estate has been and continues to be a solid investment. They're not just making a loan; they're using the property as collateral. If something goes wrong, and you have to default, the lender gets to foreclose on the property. It reduces their risk significantly.

This is a pretty easy way to fund a deal, but it's also one of the more expensive ways to borrow money too. We typically pay between 10% and 12% depending on the lender when funding deals this way. At 12% per annum, or 1% per month. You'd have to pay $500 every month if you borrowed $50,000. That can be quite a bit of money out of your pocket until you're able to refinance that property. We can't stress this enough; you have to know your numbers when you are doing the BRRRR strategy. Holding costs can add up, so you have to know what your holding costs are going to be. For example, if you're going to hold that $50,000 loan for six months, then you'd have to calculate six months' worth of holding costs. That's $3000 just for that loan. If you know your numbers, and they make sense, private lending one to one, is a pretty easy way to do it.

Private money is when you know someone that has money they're willing to invest. They might not want to buy a home or manage a portfolio themselves. They want to lend it to someone at a fixed interest rate, so they know the money is coming in without them having to work for it. If you borrowed from a private lender, you could take that money, buy a house, rehab it and get a refinanced loan from a bank. Then you take the original sum of money you owe the private money lender and pay it back. There are lots of private money lenders. A great place to meet them is at local REIA's. We went to one just last week. By the end of it, we had four or five different people handing out business cards, telling us that they're hard money lenders, or private money investors.

Hard Money

Another type of private lender is called a hard money lender. There's a slight distinction between private money and hard money, although they're similar. A hard money lender is a lender that lends money on a hard asset like real estate. In order for them to want to lend their money they need to know the deal is going to make a profit. If you can find a good deal, show them that you can add value by fixing it, and sell it for a profit, they're going to want a piece of that profit. A private lender is usually doing this as a one off, or less formally. They typically charge a bit less than a formal hard money lender. A hard money lender probably has an established business or LLC dedicated to lending money.

Hard Money lenders are typically more institutional then individual. They do this as a business and charge fees or points, but really evaluate the deal more than a regular person. It's really that easy. When times are good, the money flows, especially if you find a good deal. Money is everywhere. When times are a little tougher, the money flows towards the better deals. So getting a discount on a property just becomes that much more important

Longhorn Investments, based in Texas, are a pretty established hard money lender in St. Louis. We would consider them an institutional investor. Hard money lenders look more at a particular asset than your creditworthiness for determining whether or not they want to grant a loan. Private money lenders come in all shapes and sizes, and each is going to have their own lending criteria. An example of a possible private money lender is a rich uncle, or maybe grandparents who have a big retirement account. There are usually friends or family members who want to invest money with you. They might be willing to lend you money because they have seen flipping houses, wholesaling, and/or renting properties and making some good money at it. You might have to get some experience before people can trust that you can make them money. But it all comes back to knowing and demonstrating that your numbers make financial sense.

Bank Funding

Third easiest route is a traditional mortgage or bank loan. With a traditional bank loan, you find a property, then talk to a mortgage broker or bank. You discuss with them your intent to buy a house. They send the loan application through underwriting and hopefully approve you to purchase the house. With this funding scenario, you're typically going to have to come up with 10-20% down. You're also most likely going to have to fund the rehab yourself. Some banks are willing to lend on the rehab costs as well. This is considered a construction loan. However, you want to make that plan very clear to the bank upfront about what you're doing. You want everyone on the same page.

W-2 jobs definitely help with getting bank loans. unless you have two to three years of a business return. It might be difficult to get a bank loan if you don't have a job. We highly recommend that if you're currently working at a job, keep working at that W-2 job until you're earning a decent enough amount from your rentals, that you'll be able to support additional loans at that point. It's very important to be 'bankable'.

If you don't have the cash, you can meet a banker and discuss getting a loan. That's what banks do. That's how they make money; they lend it to people. Most people don't have $100k laying around to just go buy a property cash. So bank loans are a more likely option. If you have a W-2 job, or you have a job that pays you a salary, that's going to help you tremendously with getting a bank loan. Most people don't realize it, but banks are more willing to give an individual with steady income five to ten loans before they'd even consider loaning to a business to buy property. Banking guidelines usually allow you to purchase up to ten properties in your name. It should be relatively easy to buy a rental property with a bank loan. You might even get the money you need to purchase it *and* to rehab it from your bank. This would be considered a construction loan. These typically come at higher interest rates, and the money is paid out as work is finished.

Line of Credit

Next form of funding would be using a revolving line of credit if you have it. Although it's a bit more complicated than the strategies we just mentioned. You have to set it up with your bank. A revolving line of credit is something you can get in your personal name or get for a business. It's a bit more of a process to set one up than getting a bank loan. However, after you set it up, you can draw from it and pay it back. It's a really great tool to fund your purchase.

The process of setting up a line of credit is pretty simple, but you're going to have to put up some form of collateral. That can be cash, a CD, real estate, or stocks. There are probably a handful of other things you could use as collateral too. The bank is going to look at how much of these assets you control compared to how much debt you have on them. In other words, how much equity you have in the assets. Then they let you borrow a percentage against that. It's usually in the 50% to 70% range. Those assets are tied up or frozen when you're using them as collateral. You can't sell them, but you can borrow against them.

The benefit to this is, as your BRRRR strategy progresses, you can start pulling equity from other assets you've owned for a long time. Now you can collect a return in two ways. You have the initial asset itself with the cash flow, and you can borrow against that to acquire more. It's a very powerful tool and it's an advanced strategy. It's not for everyone, because you need assets or equity in properties to make it happen. However, it's super easy to use. It's one of the best tools that we have.

Private Equity Fund

The next would be a private equity fund. This is above our pay grade. We have not done this with our company, but we thought we should mention it. We looked into it and we have friends that do a lot of them. It was more complicated than we wanted to deal with. In anycase, a private equity fund is when you try to raise X amount of money from multiple people.

Pooling money can get tricky from a legal standpoint. In fact, you might not even be able to call it pooling. It might go by a different name. When you start mixing different people's money together to buy an asset, it muddies the water for litigation. Essentially the fund owns that asset, and people own shares of the fund. We have a course called Savvy Leverage, that describes this in further detail. Visit DPIPodcast.com -> Go to Tool Kit -> Then Go to Course Catalog to find this course.

We partnered with our buddy Dan Gibson. Now he's got multiple million-dollar funds. He does a great job. You can fly a little bit safer under the SEC if you have funds less than a million versus over a million. There are different types of funds, and there are different regulations. Typically, anything under a million dollars is going to be a little bit easier. It can be complicated. If you feel like this is a strategy for you, you definitely need to educate yourself before jumping in.

Private money 2.0 is when you create a fund. We have a course on this called Savvy Leverage. You can pool together money from up to 25 different people. You can then use this fund to buy properties. http://dpipodcast.com/funding/

Subject-To

The next one is referred to as subject-to. We've done a couple of subject-to deals. Subject-to is an interesting way to buy a property. We've even wholesaled some properties subject-to. When you acquire a property subject-to, you're buying subject-to the existing mortgage. The name subject-to is just a shortened phrase for buying a property with the existing mortgage in place.

To do it, you have to find a motivated seller that is willing to let you take over their payments. You need to describe the process and show them that you're trustworthy enough to continue making their payments. Since the property is being bought subject-to the existing mortgage, their name will still be on the mortgage. If you stop making these payments it will screw up their credit, and the house could be lost by both parties. When you take over these payments, you usually do it with an agreement to close out the loan or pay it off within a certain time frame, generally three to five years.

Given the risk, you might ask yourself why anyone would sell via subject-to. Usually the seller just wants to not have to pay the mortgage anymore. They're willing to walk away from equity, if there is any, for their convenience. For a buyer, it can be a great deal, especially if you don't have the money for a down payment, creditworthiness, or a W-2 for a bank loan. You take over the payments, put a renter in place, and profit from the spread between the rent and payments. It's a win-win for both parties.

With a subject-to deal, you're going to be talking directly to the seller. You're most likely not going to be able to pick up one of these deals off the MLS. This is where wholesale marketing really comes into play. If you're not marketing, you're not going to have motivated sellers, or off market property owners contacting you to sell you their homes. You're just not going to come across these types of deals.

We have a friend Jeff Coffman, that we did an episode on the DPI Podcast with. He used the subject-to strategy to flip properties. He would take over payments for people that have properties with some equity. Then he'll spend his own money rehabbing the unit to increase the value. After it's fixed up, he'll sell off the property, pay off the loan and profit from the spread. It's an interesting strategy. Subject-to, is simply a buying strategy for acquiring property subject-to the existing mortgage.

Seller Carry Back Loan

A Seller carry back loan is somewhat similar to subject-to. You're going to be dealing directly with a seller on these deals too. These cases usually have the property free and clear though. I.e. They don't have a loan on it. They might be trying to get a little more money for their property by not selling it for cash. They are financing the property. The seller is basically the lender on the property. You create a note with them, and they act as the bank for the property. You send them payments each month instead of the bank.

There are advantages to this strategy for both the buyer and the seller side. As the buyer, you're getting a loan from the seller. You're not having to go to a private lender, a bank, or use your own cash. You're simply getting a loan from the seller. There are several benefits for the seller too. They can sell you a house at market price or near market price. Although they aren't going to get cashed out right away, they stand to make more money in the long run. Another advantage is a tax advantage. People who have owned these houses for a very long time have depreciated these houses on their taxes down to zero. So when they sell, they're going to have to pay a major tax bill. If they loan you the money over a longer period of time, it reduces their taxable income.

Lease Options

Last but not least is the common strategy of lease option. You can buy or sell a property with a lease option. A lease option is where you lease a property from the owner, but you also have the option to purchase it at a later date for a specified price. That price is agreed upon by both you and the seller. You also make an agreement on the lease duration and price. You can negotiate X number of months or years. The option gives you the ability to buy it at a set price within a specified time frame.

There are advantages to doing these. If you're on the buying side, you can use a lease option to buy a property with little to no money. You can do this by re-leasing the property to a tenant and using the money they give you to pay the lease, and you keep the spread. When you're selling, you typically make more money selling a deal like that, because you're giving the buyer some flexibility. You give them a chance to save up some money for a down payment if they don't already have it. You're giving them the ability to work with you. Lease options are a great strategy. We've done a whole podcast on it with Gavin, and even one with Joe. There are probably several other podcasts out there that we have done personally that talk about the advantages of lease options and how they work.

Recap:

1. **Cash:** If you have access to it, this is the quickest and easiest way to fund a purchase.

2. **Private Funding:** Private funding creates a win-win scenario between you and the lender. You can often give them a higher interest rate than their other investments, and you get to purchase a property without using a bank.

3. **Hard Money:** This is very similar to private money, but this usually refers to a more institutional lender.

4. **Bank Funding:** This is traditional funding and is subject underwriter approval. You generally have to put 10-20% down.

5. **Line of Credit:** It takes some effort to set up but is a useful tool. This allows you to borrow the equity from your properties or other assets used as collateral.

6. **Private Equity Fund:** This is beyond our pay grade; however, we have friends that use this method. It involves pooling money, and can get a bit tricky, so make sure you follow the regulations on this.

7. **Subject-To:** This is basically just taking over the mortgage payments and can be a great way to get a property without having to get a loan.

8. **Seller Carry Back Loan:** With this strategy, the seller acts as the bank. They provide you the loan for the property.

9. **Lease Option:** This gives you the option to buy a property for an agreed upon price at a later date. Meanwhile, you can put a renter in there while you're leasing it and make money off the spread.

Don't let money stop you. Don't spend six months trying to get money before you start looking for deals. It takes a while to get your deal funnel going. You need to be following up and building it. Deals sell themselves. If you find a deal, you should be able to talk to other investors at a REIA club and find a buyer. Or you can find a private lender or hard money lender. If you show them that you have a deal, they'll throw money your way trying to get paid a healthy interest rate.

Money is actually one of the easiest things to get, once you have a deal.

It behooves you to start wholesaling first. Start your marketing efforts now to find off market properties and motivated sellers. It's a great way to make money and get experience. Learning how to market for motivated sellers is one of the most important things you can do in your real estate investing career. Know your numbers. If you have a deal that has good numbers, funding your purchase should be easy. Another option for funding your deals is available at www.DPIPodcast.com/funding where we have a partner show you how to utilize 0% credit cards to fund your business up to $250,000.

Action Item: Start talking to friends and family about your real estate business. Tell them about how you buy property, and how private lending works. Discussing money can make some people uncomfortable, so we suggest you make it a practice to stretch your comfort zone and talk about money and real estate. This is not meant to be a hard sell, but rather, treat it as an opportunity to educate people on their options. You never know who has money or is willing to lend it until you start talking about it.

"Everyone must choose between one of two pains: The pain of discipline or the pain of regret." -Jim Rohn

CHAPTER 10

Case Study: 974 Lindsay

L et's talk a little bit about the way we purchase our rentals, and the way we are funding these deals. We love educating the new investor on how to get started in real estate with little to no money. Wholesaling is our bread and butter because of the quick cash, and how we can make money while using little to none of our own money. However, now we've been amassing a pretty decent rental portfolio to build wealth and get massive passive cash flow. So, we would like to teach you how we apply the strategy of using little to no money to acquiring and rehabbing rental properties. There's no reason an investor can't switch their investing strategy as they gain experience. Someone might dabble in wholesaling (which is where we suggest you start), and say, "You know what? With my personality, I don't think I'm a wholesaler. I don't like it. I want more hands-on work. I want the big checks like the rehabbers. Or I want to build wealth and passive income."

These real estate strategies work well together, and they work well separately. Hopefully, if you're reading this book, you fit this rehab then rental model. We're good at it because we're pretty detail orientated. We enjoy looking at the numbers, keeping the projects on track, and keeping the budget low. It's a fun game that suits our personalities. There is a lot of tracking if you want to be successful. You've got to be a really organized individual to make this business work.

Let's give some advice for the person who is just starting out. How do you buy a rental with no money? You might not know this yet, but there are plenty of different ways to acquire funding to build your rental portfolio without using your own money. It's very possible. On our podcast, we talked about private money. But we were not really using it as much, at least not in our company. We had done a couple of deals in the past, but our company wasn't fully utilizing it, or at least not to the extent we could have. There are people with money out there. We know people with money. We're friends with other real estate investors who have money. It's not a big deal. We often see in new investors, the topic of money, being a big block in people's minds. They're wondering, "How do I get money?" The money is out there. There is so much money out there. It's just a matter of finding someone willing to let you use it. Trust us, there are people that you know that have got money sitting in a bank account, and they want to earn interest on it.

They're going to be making a lot more money by lending it to you, or us, than letting it sit in a bank, or putting it into CD's. Having said that, people who earned and saved their money aren't fools. They didn't amass their wealth by gambling it away. They're not going to just give you money because you asked. It's your job to show them how their wealth is protected, and what's in it for them. Stocks and other asset classes can come with their own risk. Real estate, historically, is a safe bet, and we'll show you how to get your message across to the would-be private money lender.

A. You bought the property at a discount

B. You are going to increase the value of it by rehabbing it

C. Their investment is backed by an asset.

The worst burn they can get is if they loan you money, and you default (stop paying them). Then they would be required to foreclose on you. But again, that property would be worth more than what they had invested because you bought it at a discount and put some work into it.

Let's talk about the property in this case study with real numbers. We bought it for $58k. We estimated the after-repair value to be $99k. To ballpark it, we bought something around $60k, and we believe it'll be worth about $100k after all is said and done. You can approach someone you know who has money or you think has money. This could be your mom/dad/aunt/uncle, whoever. Just approach them and ask them for money using the bullet points we listed above. Again, this is private money lending. These are people you know. There are rules when it comes to asking to borrow money. You can't just approach strangers and ask to borrow money, especially if you're pooling the money (putting different people's money into one fund). That's something you'd really have to research and is beyond the scope of this book.

However, if you know anyone, including another real estate investor, or a hard money lender, you just need to justify your numbers, so it makes sense for them to lend. Hard money lenders tend to be pretty tight with their numbers, and they would probably lend on a project like this.

We just approach people we know, and say to them, "Hey, we can get you a higher interest on your money, and this is what we're doing...." And then go into your spiel with the bullet points we listed above.

By the way, hard money just means their money is backed by a hard money asset. In this case, real estate. A private lender is a hard money lender. Having said that, there are hard money lenders that use hard money as a full-scale business. They can charge points down and some really high interest rates. But they're out there for the people who need to use them.

When someone is lending money on a property their risk is secured by the first lien. It is recorded against the property. A person cannot sell the property without paying back the loan. When you go to closing, you are signing a promissory note, agreeing to pay them, at whatever terms you negotiated.

In the event that we were not able to pay them back, they can foreclose because they have that first lien. This is just like how a bank would foreclose on someone if they didn't pay their mortgage. We essentially have a mortgage with our private lender. The terms you negotiate with your lender before closing on the property. And that's part of the paperwork given to you at closing. If it's a family member or a friend, whoever; you can negotiate favorable terms. Maybe you don't want to have to pay monthly payments. You could negotiate terms to where you pay when you sell or refinance the property in 6 months. You can pay 5% or 10% or whatever works for every party involved. That's the great thing about these. You can negotiate how you want to pay them back, how you're going to pay them back, and how much interest or points you want to pay. It's all negotiable and can work out really well for everyone involved.

So back to the case study, we borrowed private money on this one. We bought it for $60k. We had an estimated after repair value (ARV) of around $100k. We estimated the repairs to be around $12k. We did a lot to this property, so $12k was a bit light of a budget. We ended up spending about $20k on this one. We went over our budget a little bit. But that's okay. We were in it for about $80k, when it's all said and done. Again, think of this through the lender's eyes. They're lending $60k and getting 5-10% for their money. Absolute worst-case scenario, they have to foreclose on us, and they get a $100k house for the $60k they lent us. It's a no brainer for them. Trust us, the money is out there if you find the deal.

We were hoping to be all in on this one at about $72k. We went ahead and rehabbed it. You can watch the video to get a better sense of how things went. It's found on FreeLandlordCourse.com in the Case Study Section. It's an interesting story, a long story, but not really important. We actually didn't really want to buy this one. But it kind of fell into our laps and we closed on it. When we bought it, there were some things that needed to be done rehab wise to make it work. There was a deck, and basement that needed work. A lot of flooring, and other issues needed to be addressed. The inspector came in and gave us a hard time on some stuff. It wasn't anything major. However, it did add to the initial scope of work though. We estimated $12k in repairs and then we had to spend $20k. That happens a lot. The inspectors come in after you've already done your repairs and used up your repair budget. Then they ask you to make additional fixes that you hoped wouldn't have to be done. They may say this deck has got to go, or you need to replace it.

The deck is one of the things on here that we left it undone because we knew there were going to be some things we needed to fix. We just said to him, "We know the deck needs work. We're going to fix it, but what do you want us to do with it? Do you want us to tear it down? Or can we replace a couple of boards?" That's a good pro tip right there. Sometimes you don't necessarily need to spend all the money preparing for the inspector. You can leave something questionable undone and ask how they'd like it done. Having a re-inspection done is cheap, in fact, the second one is included for free since it's assumed you won't pass the first time.

Instead of spending more money in the beginning trying to please an inspector; oftentimes it's best to leave a couple of things off the work order that you are kind of iffy about. Let the inspector tell you what you need to do. If you go ahead and replace the deck boards in this example on this deck, it's very possible he tells you to rip the deck down anyways. Then you've spent money replacing something that is worthless. That's frustrating. Things like that can wreck your budget. You can't control or predict what an inspector might require, or what problems you might run across during a rehab. However, you can control your expectations, how you react to situations, as well minimizing your risk by the strategy we just outlined. This property has now been rehabbed. We went a little over budget. However, our ARV was estimated at $99-100k. Now we've got the property rehabbed, a tenant in place, and the property appraised. We are in the process of refinancing.

Here's the good news, our final appraisal came back at $115k. We only estimated $99k on the ARV. You can check out the video. We did a nice job on that rehab. So even though we overspent a bit. It came back to us in equity as a higher appraised value. The appraisal was much higher than we anticipated, which is nice.

It's an interesting property. There's three bedrooms upstairs, one bath upstairs, and a bonus bedroom down in the basement. Again, we can't legally call it a bedroom. It will be advertised as office space or something else. It is a bonus though and gives the tenant options on how to best utilize the extra space. We're all into this property for about $80k. When we get an 80% loan on the $115k we'll be able to pull out that full $80k. We'll be able to get all of our money back, as well as having some equity built up.

We could be really aggressive and try to get all the money back out of it. The math comes out at $115k times 80% and gives us $92k. We could do that. However, our goal is to maximize cash flow and build equity. It's not always in our best interest to fully leverage properties. We are just trying to get our money back, that's the name of the game. If we don't have to borrow the 80%, we can borrow 75-77%, or even 70% if that suits us. Again, there's two games you're playing with the rentals, which is cash flow and that equity pick up. Both are important.

We're playing both of those games now, and again, we want you guys to learn how to do that as well. The moral of the story on this one is that you don't have to have money to buy the rentals. Get connected with other investors, ask them how they are doing it. Go to your real estate meetups and ask around. Become friends with people that are already successful in this business. Find out who has money sitting around. If they have an IRA, a 401k, or money sitting around, they might be ready to invest. We have some money sitting right now that's not even invested. A lot of people out there do. We would much rather earn 7-8% over a three to six-month term, than zero. Why not? If you buy right, and follow the system we've laid out, the people you borrow from are going to earn more than that. Those loans are only over three to six months. As you develop a proven track record, more people with more money will be interested in lending to you. Right now, a pretty standard rate for CD's is producing 1-2% per year. We can offer up to 1% a month which comes out to 12% a year. It's pretty good money to loan it out. If you have money, loan it out. If you need money, borrow it.

*** Walk Through***

*** Visit www.FreeLandLordCourse.com***

Go to the case study section to watch this video

Welcome back. We are at 974 Lindsay Lane. We got this one for a really good price. We're trying to max out the ARV with a rehab. Our strategy is to purchase the property, rehab it, rent it, then refinance with the bank to get most of our money back. Then we will hold it as a rental. We bought this property for $58k. We're pretty much done, just got to put on some finishing touches. You can see that we've still got to glue the end cap to the edge of the countertop. Other than that, we did a pretty solid job on the kitchen. It looks really good. Most of these cabinets were in here already. There was a cabinet piece sticking out into the kitchen. We moved it over to the far side, and bought an upper cabinet set. With that, we were able to create this additional workspace, as well as opening up the kitchen or dining area.

The cabinets were solid, but looked old, we painted them white. This is a pretty standard operating procedure for us. If the cabinets are solid wood, we like to keep them and freshen them up a bit. Some paint and new handles give them that fresh and clean look. With our stainless-steel appliances, it really makes everything pop. This kitchen is going to make it an easy house to rent out at the top of market rent. We're probably going to get at least $1200 for this. We're asking $1295, so we'll see what happens.

The floor is something we really like. This is a rubber backed vinyl that basically clicks together. It's kind of like the old Pergo style flooring that just clicks together. This vinyl floor is easy to cut. We picked it up at $1.99 per square foot from a local hardware store. This is one of our bigger expenses in the house. We paint all the walls in the house an agreeable grey and use white trim. We use very similar, if not exactly the same material in many of our other rental properties. We use the same ceiling fans in every property, and they cost $59. We've got a ceiling fan in the dining area, and a track light in the kitchen. There was hardwood throughout the house. A lot of these older houses have hardwood. Sometimes it's under the carpet. Quick tip, you can often pull up a bit of carpet not tacked down by removing a floor register and pulling it up a couple inches. This allows you to take a peek under the carpet to see if there's hardwood underneath without removing or damaging any carpet. This is a great tip for before you buy a house to get a sense of what you're working with. Having said that, you don't know it's true condition until the carpet is removed. And you can't do that until you own the house.

For this project all we had to do was pull off the quarter round around the rooms that had hardwood. Quarter round is an extension of the base board and hides the edges of the wood flooring. That still needs to go back. After the contractors pulled off the quarter round, they refinished the hardwood floors. Now they have to put the quarter round back down to finish it up. We refinished the hardwood floors throughout the whole upstairs. It's not cheap, and can have a decent cost to it, but it's worth it.

Let's talk about the bathroom now. There are a couple things we did to the bathroom. On the floor we used peel and stick tile. It's about two bucks per square foot as well. It's also easier to install than traditional tile. For this project, we opted for a double sink. The plumbing was suited for it, but we did need a much larger vanity since there was room for it. This is a good-sized bathroom, and the renters will get a nice vanity. We're trying to get the most we can out of the ARV on this one. We have a nice light fixture and didn't go cheap on our mirror. The mirror looks great. There's an outlet here that we were conscious to not cover up.

This tile is not new. It was an old 50's style green. We have a guy that we use to glaze it. He comes in and scrubs it all clean, makes sure everything is patched up, then puts a nice durable paint on it that isn't going to chip off. It really looks brand new from where we're standing. The only reason you could tell it's not new is if you saw it before. There's another option we're going to start doing in more of our rental properties. Using an oil-based paint sticks really well. After that, put a coat of polyurethane on top of it to help protect it so it lasts longer and doesn't chip.

We had to replace all the doors. We go with six panel doors everywhere. The bedroom is pretty basic. We have white trim, an agreeable grey paint, and we refinished the hardwood floors, and added a nice ceiling fan. Everything we use gives a nice clean fresh look. That was bedroom one. One of the main reasons we really liked this property was what they did to this house. They built a deck off the back of the house. Both back bedrooms have doors that can walk onto the deck on the back. Both of the back bedrooms are really bright. Without the blinds, it makes the bedrooms and the deck both look that much bigger. Pretty nice feature of this house.

We haven't redone the deck yet. We left it undone on purpose because we have to get an occupancy inspection. Inspectors are notorious for requesting investors to fix things, even when we do our best to put out a quality product. We know they're going to ding us for something. So rather than fixing the deck and hoping it passes, we are going to wait and ask him what he wants us to do with the deck. We are planning on just replacing a few boards and painting it. Hopefully that's all we have to do. There's a chance he walks out there and tells us we need to re-brace it or worse, rebuild the deck. If that's the case we're wasting time and money by replacing the boards and painting them. On cases like these, it's best to make sure that you're on the same page with the inspector before you invest a lot of money for no reason. So, we are going to take our time with that.

There was a bedroom with a huge section of hardwood that was just destroyed. We have photos and will put those up for you. Our flooring guy did a great job of replacing the boards. When they refinish the floor, it's almost impossible to tell that anything has been done.

We've covered the kitchen, the family room, the bedrooms, and upstairs bathroom. The basement is what we're really proud of. The contractors did a great job. The flooring is the same as upstairs. We like to keep it the same everywhere. When we replace parts of it or go onto the next project, we have the same materials. It takes out the guesswork, and we don't have to keep returning materials after a project is done. We like to use river birch flooring. Next project, we'll have a couple of extra boxes ready to go. We buy more and it gets used.

Before the rehab this backspace was used as a storage area. It was unfinished. What we did was put a wall up and added a door to create a nice office, separating it from the back storage-space. It's a good-sized room. It doesn't technically qualify as a bedroom because we don't have an egress up here. We can't advertise it as a bedroom, but we can call it an office. An egress is an opening, usually a door or window for someone to exit in case there's a fire. Someone could essentially turn it into a bedroom. We Just can't legally call it that for the occupancy inspection or appraisal. The inspector will come in and measure the bedrooms and tell us how many people are allowed to live in the house. Typically, they allow for two individuals per bedroom. We can have up to six people on the occupancy permit for this three-bedroom house. But as we mentioned, they could use this area as an additional bedroom if they want.

This house does have a walkout basement in one of the storage areas, which is nice. There's a walkout basement, and we've got a fun little bathroom back here. It's a 3/4 bathroom with a sink, toilet, and a shower. It's back here, and usable. It really makes that bonus room or office space more attractive. It'll most likely be used as a bedroom and adds a lot more value.

In the back storage-space, we didn't do much other than paint the walls. We just use Kilz to paint the walls. The furnace is a bit older but it's probably going to get us by. Again, this was a really inexpensive purchase for us. The water heater is back here. It's hard to see because there's not much light, but it looks good. It's in decent shape, and nothing we are too worried about. We have two good storage rooms down here. In this one, we didn't paint the walls, we just painted the floor back there because of the utility systems. It just makes it look nice and clean. That's a wrap on 974 Lindsay Lane.

PART III

REHAB

CHAPTER 11

Why Rehab?

Why You Have to Rehab

This chapter is about rehabbing. We're going to chop it into 3 smaller segments. We're going to focus on how rehabbing for your rental properties differs from doing a major flip or rehab on your own house. We'll discuss the differences and the reasons we make the decisions we do.

You have two options. You can do all the work in the beginning when the unit is vacant. Or you can do the minimal work to get it up to code, but then you're going to be coming back a lot to do repairs. We prefer to do all the necessary repairs right from the beginning. We're not able to eliminate maintenance altogether. However, our goal is to do as much as we can in the beginning to prevent or reduce maintenance down the road.

It's a win-win situation. It's a win for you because you're not having to deal with a bunch of pesky repair calls. And it's a win for the tenant because your tenants don't want to deal with repairs either. They would rather live and stay in a nice clean place for the most part. The final win is for you again. The refinance portion of BRRRR is where you get your money back. You spend the money up front. Then when you refinance, you don't actually have as much money in the property anyways. Then you can cash flow with an asset with little to no money invested in it, while building equity.

You might ask yourself, "Why would you invest more money into a property that you are going to have as a rental? Why not just buy a house that's already nice?" That's a great question. But before we jump into that, we want to recap what the BRRRR strategy is. It stands for Buy, Rehab, Rent, Refinance, Repeat. Everyone of these steps in this process is very, very important.

In order for you to rent out a property after you purchase it, 9 out of 10 times you're going to have to rehab it in some regard by default just to get it to rent ready condition. Not to mention, a big reason why we can buy properties at a discount is because they often need a lot of work. The rehab is also needed for you to get a refinance rate that is favorable, so you can continue the BRRRR strategy. You have to rehab the property. If you're buying a property that doesn't need a rehab, it's going to be very difficult to convince your banking partners to give you a refinance to where you can get all or most of your money back.

Let's say we purchased a property that needs some work. This is also a big part of why we can buy them at a discount, because they need rehabbing. It's really kind of a requirement for us to use the BRRRR strategy to its fullest potential. When we are able to buy at a discount and do a significant rehab, we're able to add value above and beyond just the material cost and effort put into those properties. For every dollar we put in we're trying to get two dollars in value metaphorically speaking.

Quick example; say we buy a property that is a little three-bedroom one-bath. It's worth around $100,000 once it's fixed up. That's what other properties in the area are selling for when they're fixed up. We are able to buy it for $60,000. The kitchen is outdated, the bathroom is outdated. It looks pretty bad. If we're able to buy it at $60,000 off market, we have a couple options. We can fluff it up. We can do a quick rental rehab on it, and maybe spend $20,000. So now we're going to be into this property for $80,000. It's going to be worth $100,000 on paper. That's a $20,000 equity capture.

Preventative Maintenance

Another reason to rehab is to make it a hassle-free unit. We've all heard that terminology of the three T's in the investing world. It's tenants, toilets, and taxes. Those are the three biggest hassles when you're a landlord and own properties. Tenants are often a hassle because they might not pay rent or have other issues. When we say "toilets" we're just talking about property maintenance. So our objective when rehabbing this unit is to make the house bullet proof. We want it to be hassle free for years. We want surfaces that wipe down easily so they're easy to clean. We want things that work. If you go cheap with the lowest grade plumbing or electric fixtures, it's probably going to be broken in four months. A cheap shower head might start leaking and spraying water before you know it. There are some of those things that it's worth it to spend the extra money on to prevent a maintenance call. Spending a couple extra bucks on a shower head or toilet is going to save a lot more money and hassle in the long run than needing to send out a handyman or a plumber just to replace a shower head.

Nice Place for Tenants

As we have mentioned before, we are always trying to create win-win relationships. The same goes for relationships with our tenants. We are rehabbing the properties not only to get a favorable bank appraisal and refinance number, but also to create a nice place for the tenant to live. To us, nice means an updated home in an area they can afford to live. Nice means we have less maintenance requests. This is a big one! Maintenance calls can be trouble for your bottom line and a big aggravation for tenants living in your houses. Think about it, you don't want to live in a house where things are constantly breaking down or broken. When rehabbing houses we like to 'bite the bullet' and pay for things that will make the home last longer without issues. These aren't necessarily the big VALUE ADDS like Remodeling a kitchens or bathrooms. We don't often knock out walls. To us, nice frequently includes putting a new roof or getting trees around the houses trimmed so they're not a nuisance. We also opt for less expensive cosmetic updates to our kitchens and baths. We can think this through a couple different ways.

Scenario 1: We replace the roof and have the trees trimmed around the house at time of rehab. If you live in the Midwest like us, it could be important to have a sump pump and drain tile put in the basement if we saw some evidence of water in the basement. We might do a light fluff up on the bathrooms and kitchen and put new luxury vinyl flooring throughout the home. We'll paint the walls and update light fixtures. Then when we refinance the property, we'll get most or all of our money back for the rehab. It might seem like we're putting a lot of money into a rental rehab, but we don't really come out of pocket for these bigger ticket items. A few months later, a storm could come in and we won't get any calls about this property. We can save our energy to continue looking for our next rental property to buy.

Scenario 2: We gut the kitchen and put in new cabinets with granite countertops and high-end appliances. We put in a high-end solid wood floor and decide to GUT the bathrooms as well. This is a common mistake for newbies. If it's your first rehab, you probably want to make it look great. It's common to blow your budget on high end fixes with this approach. Now you might be thinking you don't need to replace the roof or trim the trees around the house. If a storm rolls through, a branch could fall on the roof putting a hole in the roof. Now the tenant's possessions are damaged by water from the storm. They're not happy about it and want you to pay for their damaged TV, furniture, or whatever else they might own. Now you have to get a hole in the roof repaired. You have to fix the drywall ceiling, and make sure there's no water damage to insulation in the attic or damage to the floor and walls inside. You might have gotten most of your cash back when you refinanced. However, if you blew your budget on bathroom and kitchen remodels, your house is over improved for the area and won't have much equity left. The roof, the tree removal, and any other fixes you'd have to make as a result of the storm damage now come out of your pocket. It'll take years or more of rent to make up for the extra improvements you did by not prioritizing them in the first place. These fixes will now have to be done on short notice. Your tenants won't like the intrusion into 'their home' and life.

This is just one example of how a long-term owner is going to look at rehabbing vs a short-term flipper. As a BRRRR investor, you want to think about long term solutions when you are REHABBING the house. It's about making it a secure and nice place to live. You're not on TV trying to maximize the WOW factor, and you're also not trying to put lipstick on a pig. You're in it for the long haul, and you need to do things right. Do the not so fun things now so you don't get stuck doing the REALLY REALLY not fun things later.

Appraisal/Refinancing

The quality of your rehab has a lot to do with the appraisal. If you only spend 3-5K on a rehab, the appraiser might not see that as much of an improvement. They're comparing your home to others in similar condition. Their opinion of the value of the home might not be high enough for you to get your money back out when you refinance. We try to spend at least $15K for the 'entrepreneurial credit'.

Our bankers tell us their requirements for the entrepreneurial credit. Your banker might have a different requirement. Before you get started, make sure you tell them you're using the BRRRR strategy. You can even tell them you learned about this strategy from David and Mike at the Discount Property Investor podcast. Maybe they'll listen to us. If they don't know much about this strategy now, they will soon learn about it. Most bankers are pretty familiar with the BRRRR strategy though. In order for them to give you a loan based on the appraisal; the bankers have to consider an entrepreneurial credit. Without spending around $15k, the bank might just refinance the property for what you have into it (purchase price and fix up costs). Entrepreneurial credit is banking language for the underwriters to do their due diligence and pay out properly (appraisal amount).

It takes time to develop a relationship with a bank. If you're just starting out with this, you might not be able to get that credit right away. It took us at least ten houses before our banker told us about this. It's kind of a hidden secret among bankers. It's definitely worth asking about when shopping around for a banker.

We didn't even realize what they were doing. They were looking at the appraisal. They always have to look at the appraisal. Then they look at what we bought it for and how much money we put into rehabbing it. They want to know all the details, so then they can figure out what to lend on the property.

It can take a while to build up that relationship before they trust that you know what you're doing. They need proof. They need a track record of payments. You are building trust with your bank. It may take five to ten units before the bank no longer looks at you as high risk. Now, as long as we can prove we spent $15,000 on the rehab, they're more willing to look past all the minor due diligence issues. Now they lend on the value of the appraisal. A lot of times we don't even want the full amount that they will lend us, because we also want to keep our equity and cash flow high. We just need to pay our lenders back.

You're not going to be able to refinance a property if it's already fixed up. Typically, when you get a loan from a bank on an investment property it's not a primary residence. It's not even a secondary home. It's an investment property. They're going to give you a loan based upon the purchase price, and the cost of those renovations. However, if you spend at least $15,000, or at least with our banking partners, they can look beyond those two numbers. They're now able to lend on the appraisal price. This is huge! It's almost magical. This is another one of those things that makes real estate such a powerful tool.

Rental Rehab vs. Retail Rehab

We want to explain the difference between some repair terms that often get thrown around and used interchangeably. We want to make the distinction as to why these terms are actually different and how that applies to BRRRR., and why we choose the repairs we make.

Restoration: This entails bringing the house back to its original condition. This is expensive and not necessary for what we do. This is typically done when taking a really old house and restoring it to its historical time period.

Remodel: This is changing the structure of the home, and often changing the use of a room or building. Walls might be torn out, plumbing, electrical work, or air ducts might be moved. An addition might be added on. This type of work is very expensive and doesn't fit our strategy either.

Rehabbing: Taking an old, outdated house, and making it more functional and livable for modern use. The idea is to make it nice and functional, not completely change what's already there. Rehab costs vary in cost and quality. As we mentioned with our description of Class A, B, C, and D areas, the idea is to keep the quality in line with typical houses of that neighborhood.

Because we're doing a quick rental fluff up, we're going to spend a bit less money than a full-blown rehab or remodel. The house is going to be used by a renter as opposed to a new home buyer. We're not going to do all the same things we would for a rehab project we're looking to sell retail. We're going to make it look good, but it doesn't have to be perfect. We're fine if it's a bit of an older roof. We don't necessarily have to replace the roof, yet we should still get a pretty similar appraisal value. Whereas if we were going to sell it, we might have to replace that roof. A 15-year-old roof probably still has half its life yet. However, a new homebuyer or inspector might point out that it's old and needs to be replaced. These are just slight differences where you can add value to the property. We want to clarify; *we are NOT encouraging you to cut corners on costly repairs now.* If you own the house for 15-20 years, you're most likely going to put that roof on at some point. If it is showing real signs of wear and tear, do it now. You might as well do it now so you can refinance that cost out. However, if it still looks good and has no evidence of leaks or roof failure, keep it.

The grade of the rehab is very important. It's going to affect the decisions you make. If you are buying a property to flip, meaning you're going to rehab it to sell it retail, then it needs to be a higher quality rehab. You're probably going to need to swap out the kitchen cabinets. But when you're dealing with a rental property, you're more concerned about condition than style. So instead of ripping those cabinets out, you could paint them or add new hardware. With rental rehabs, there's definitely corners you can cut, or costs that you can avoid.

We just walked through one of our properties yesterday where the cabinets looked great. However, if you looked up underneath the sink, it was all rotted. Because it was a rental, we decided not to replace the whole cabinet. We're going to find and fix the leak, cut out the boards underneath the sink, and replace those boards. Once we paint them, they'll look brand new. We've actually seen people use a plastic tray with PVC as a cheap and easy fix for rotted cabinet boards.

There's lots of little tips and tricks to save money. We're not saying you should cut corners to deliver a less than quality product. However, it's not necessary to spend crazy money on a rental property either.

These properties are going to be tenant occupied properties. There are some tips and tricks that go into rehabbing these properties. You want them to be nice, but you don't want to overdo them. You want to use materials that will stand the test of time. Select neutral colors that make them look clean. Use the same color for walls, and same color for trim and doors. We use "anew gray" for walls and a white semi-gloss for trim and doors. We suggest you KEEP THE SAME PAINT COLOR CODE for all your rentals. This will make it easy to turn over a unit when a vacancy happens. Having the same paint can save you from having to repaint an entire house to maybe just touching up a few spots. You also want durable materials that can withstand several tenants for several years, to save you the cost of having to do this every couple of years. For instance, the new "luxury" vinyl floors (LVT) we've been using for years and we expect it will last several tenants before we have to replace it. While carpet may be cheaper today it would cost us longer vacancy time when we have to turn over the property. There would be more out of pocket cost with each turn over.

You also want materials that won't be outdated in two to three years. We select neutral colors and styles as much as we can. Remember, you are not trying to create a space you love and want to love and live in. You want to update the house, and make it look modern. Occasionally, if we see a discounted item or out of box material at a steep discount, we may go for that. If we can get a higher end product (like solid wood vanity for instance) at the same cost or less than the cheaper particle board options at most big box hardware stores, then we'll choose that option. Same thing goes for light fixtures. We love getting ceiling fans in rentals because we find really good deals on them, and they seem to be a bit of luxury in some rentals. A $59 ceiling fan at Lowes may be $30 more than the globe light but adds a bit of value. It'll come back to us with a higher rent and appraisal. One ceiling fan might not make a difference, but the entirety of the finished product that will make a difference. If you like shopping for bargains this can be one of the more fun parts of the job. It's really fun finding good deals on things.

Know Your Area

Know your area. Why does that matter? As we mentioned, our goal is to do a rehab to increase the property value. The appraiser is going to look at comparable properties in the neighborhood. Every city in America is going to have nice parts of town and lower end parts of town. You want your rehab to match the condition of homes in that area that are going to comp out higher.

For example, in St Louis, Missouri, the area called north county is really great for rental properties. The numbers seem to work there more than any other part of the metro area. When we buy these houses, we're not spending $50k or $80k on the rehabs. We're generally spending $15-25K on average. Other areas will require a more expensive rehab to get a property in the same condition as it's neighbors. The reason we buy in north county and south city, is in these areas we can buy, rehab, and rent with numbers that work well for us. We use $100K ARV as an easy numbers example on the podcast all the time. However, that's not too far off from what we're looking for. We usually buy properties with ARV's around $90-120K and we're looking to purchase them around $45-70K. As the market continues its slow rise, we have to get more creative on finding deals and rehabbing for most cost-effective value addition.

When rehabbing for retail sale the quality of the rehab can vary compared to a buy and hold rental. Typically, we stay away from low-end and high-end rentals and shoot for mid-grade rehabs. This is more likely those B and C grade properties. We will do some extra things like put cages on the exterior AC units on the C grade properties and on multi-family properties in C grade. This is just protection to keep them from getting stolen. In these rougher areas we put up "video monitoring systems". By that we mean we put up fake video cameras with a flashing light and some signs that say premises under video surveillance. We stay away from the D grade areas. No amount of precautions are really going to secure your property. The way we look at it, if you wouldn't want to live in the area because of high theft and crime, then you don't want to invest there either. Your bank probably won't want too much debt in that area either. On the flip side we also don't invest in Class A areas, because those rentals won't build wealth or create good cash flow. With A-Class properties, we typically cannot buy, rehab, and make sufficient cash flow while leaving little or no money in the house. Those are okay if you're leaving lots of money in the house or have different objectives than us. Those properties make more sense to rehab for retail sale. Nicer or more expensive areas may make sense for you depending on your goals.

Know Your Numbers

Hate to beat a dead horse, but it all comes back to knowing your numbers. Whether it's wholesaling, rehabbing, or renting, it's difficult to be successful if you don't know your numbers. Wholesaling is a great way to cut your teeth and learn your numbers. When other people are walking through properties with you, or giving you feedback on pricing and condition, you'll find out really quickly whether your numbers are accurate. The hard truth is, until you do your first rehab or two, you just don't have real world experience on how repair costs seem to add up. Our goal is to provide you with as much value as we can, and hopefully keep you from making the bigger and more costly mistakes.

We want to have a rent that is going to pay the mortgage, the property manager, taxes, insurance, and save up for a repair reserve or vacancies. We

"Whether it's wholesaling, rehabbing, or renting, it's difficult to be successful if you don't know your numbers."

just want to make a little bit of cash when all is said and done. If we take out a really big mortgage, we may not be able to have that cash flow. It doesn't make sense from our perspective either to borrow more than we need.

All of these numbers have to balance out. The purchase and rehab i.e. the "all in cost", the monthly mortgage and expense, and the rent collected. It's a balancing game. If you go over your rehab number can you make it up with little higher rent? If not maybe you have to leave a little bit of money "in the property" by taking out a smaller loan on refi to decrease that monthly payment. In order to figure out where your money is going and to try and stay on budget you want to set a priority list for projects. Figure out what is absolutely needed for the occupancy permit, and if you need to get an occupancy inspection in your area. Make sure you have firm bids on or have that work completed first.

For example, the electric service lines to the house may be hanging too low. If it's under 10 feet high, it's going to feel like you can reach up and touch it. That is something you have to take care of. It's not fun money to spend, but it is absolutely necessary. So first, take care of the safety and occupancy items. Then take care of the deferred maintenance items, like a leaky roof or old HVAC systems. It's also not fun rehabbing those things because they can be expensive, but that will cut down on maintenance calls later on. Finally, you can get to work on cosmetic improvements. Paint and Light fixtures are inexpensive and make things look a lot better. Next in your budget would be the big items like flooring, kitchen cabinets, and bathroom updates.

A recent property we rehabbed we underestimated the cost of a rehab. It happens to us too. We bought an older home that needed siding and a new roof and we spent almost double what we thought we would spend on those items. Quite often, old houses are built with different construction quality than you're expecting. It's easy to get burned when things don't go the way you planned it. It was one thing after another, and it ate up almost all of our budget. So instead of doing full gut in the bathrooms and kitchen, we had to cut something out. Instead of having our floors professionally sanded and refinished we bought a product called MinWax Polystain, which is a stain and polyurethane combination. We had our painters clean the floor and paint it on. The floors turned out okay. They're not great, but it cost about $500 instead of $2000. This is just one thing we did to get back on budget. We used old appliances from another project we had going. We didn't remove an old shed from the backyard and we didn't put up a fence around the yard. All these things are minor and like mentioned above we got a new roof on and that should prevent future issues and damage to the property.

Recap:

1. **Why You Have To Rehab:** For the BRRRR model to work, you have to rehab. Most properties sold at a discount are in some disrepair anyways. This gives you the opportunity to do some preventative maintenance, and raise the value of the home.

2. **Preventative Maintenance:** We're investing in the long term, and it's easier to do necessary maintenance up front to avoid problems in the future.

3. **Nice Place For Tenants:** We seek win-win relationships in every aspect of our business, this includes our tenants. We consider them clients, and want them to have a nice place, so they'll be clients for longer.

4. **Appraisal/Refinancing:** It's important to fix the property up in such a way that you increase the appraisal value, while keeping enough equity to refinance. You want to pay back your lenders. Spending about $15k allows us to get the "entrepreneurial credit."

5. **Rental Rehab vs. Retail Rehab:** It's important to match your rehab to other houses in the area. We're also rehabbing to hold long term rather than a quick flip for cash.

6. **Know Your Area:** Class A (high end) areas tend to not cash flow well. Class D (low end) areas are often more trouble than they're worth. Class B and C areas are the goldilocks zone. Find the areas that work for you and your numbers.

7. **Know Your Numbers:** BRRRR is a balancing act. You need to buy at a discount and stay on budget to pull your money out. The property also has to cash flow after the refinance.

Action Item: Have a plan in place for rehab projects. What kind of numbers do you need to get for BRRRR to work for you and your area? Create an excel spreadsheet and get comfortable with different calculations, and the balancing act of getting the numbers right. Ask other investors how much they spend on their properties and rehabs, and what kind of cash flow they receive after refinancing.

"Every master was once a disaster." - T. Harv Eker

CHAPTER 12

Property Walk Through

This chapter is about rental rehab strategy. We're going to give you some tips and considerations through hypothetical scenarios. Let's assume we found a house we plan on holding as a rental. Next, we walk around the property, and try to figure out all the things we need to do to make this property look nice and welcoming. We want it safe for the potential tenant, and last but not least, pass an occupancy inspection. We have to pass the occupancy inspection so we can do it legally. Plus, as we mentioned, our goal in rehabbing the property is to make sure it appraises high enough to meet our needs for the refinance.

When we put together a plan for that rehab, it's going to be in conjunction with our entire plan. We make a decision of what we need to have the appraisal be before we start the rehab. In order for us to get a loan on 70-80% of the value of the home.

We need to do the rehab strategically to where we can get all of our money back. That's the reason we use the BRRRR strategy. We borrow a small amount of money to buy a property, rehab it, get it rented, refinance, then we take all of that money and pay back our private investors. We basically get a rental property for free. Which is an asset by the way, not a liability. We're getting all of our money back, yet we're controlling the asset. So it's super important to plan the rehab in a way that gets us the final number that we need. Depending on your goals and cash position you may not want to get all the money back or fully leverage the property.

Let's say we bought a house, and the numbers make sense. We bought it at a great price. We know we need to spend at least $15,000 on the rehab in order to get the entrepreneurial credit. This is a big part of our strategy. We need it to refinance the property properly. So, we walk around and start taking notes. Here is a tip, we love the notes app for this. We're Apple guys, and the notes app is great; you just open it up and hit that little microphone button. Android users most likely have a very similar thing. Evernote is also similar, but you have to pay for that. At this point, we almost all have smartphones in our pockets. In fact, that's probably how most of our students listen to our podcast (and the audio version of this book).

Outside the House

We use the notes app and start with the address. Then we walk around the property and take notes on the phone. It's not hard, take notes on your phone. It's super easy, super-fast, and saves you from having all that paper. It definitely helps us stay organized. Organization is one of the most important things in project management. We usually start by walking around the exterior. More often than not, there's a lot of old plants, bushes, and weeds that are overgrown. Overgrown vegetation is usually pretty easy to deal with. You can do it yourself or hire a landscaper. Either way, just get the overgrown vegetation removed and clean it up. To get a yard looking super clean and nice is usually not very expensive. We definitely don't need to go and buy 50 plants and redo everything. Remember, this is a rental; we just want to clean it up or remove it. If you have to put down some mulch that's fine, mulch is cheap. But we're really looking to spend the least amount of money possible to make it look it's best. We want the highest and best use of what I already have. Our goal isn't beautiful. Our goal is appealing. We do not spend any extra money on the outside that isn't necessary. Some things like replacing a retaining wall or cutting down a rotted-out tree might be necessary of course. But, a good rule of thumb is if it's not broken don't fix it.

Next we look at the roof and gutters because if they're not up to snuff, the inspector will flag those items. If there's a hole in the roof, we're going to have to fix that, before we can get an occupancy permit. If the gutters are hanging off the house, that's going to be an issue. That's probably going to lead to a flooded basement. Aside from the inspection, we want to mitigate any possible water damage before it happens. Even if the gutters aren't falling off, they could be clogged or have stuff growing out of them. So we want to clean out the gutters too. We want to make sure they're attached correctly and that the down spots are connected and the water coming through them is diverted away from the foundation of the property. Here in St Louis, basements are really common, so we want to keep the water out of the basements. Even if the property is on a slab, we'll still make sure the gutters are working correctly because we don't want water underneath the foundation. This could cause the foundation to crack or get in the house.

Most of the things we just described can be fixed for under a thousand bucks if you pay somebody to do it. These fixes are easy, so don't overthink it. Throwing down some mulch and ornamental plants a week before we have an open house for our rentals makes it look really nice and easy to rent. Little details like that make it a place that somebody wants to move into. If there's a rusty fence, a cheap way to fix that is spray paint. Or just take it out. We like to keep them if possible, because of pets. People love their pets. You open up your options to more tenants if you allow pets. Plus you can get a little bit more pet rent if there is a fence there. It makes it more welcoming not just for the tenant, but for the inspector too. You don't want them to flag it on their inspection and ask you to rip the whole thing out and redo it. That would be costly to do that. Also, you want to keep the neighbors happy.

Homeowners in a given neighborhood don't want junky rental properties near them. Nobody wants to live near that. Make it look nice and clean up everything on the outside.

Windows are something we consider to be an outside fix. We take note of the condition of the windows, when we do our outside walk around. In our opinion, if the home has older windows you should replace those. However, this can be a pricey update. It can depend on your budget whether or not it is worth it to do this. We've gone over how important it is to know your area that you're buying in. If that area doesn't have all new windows in all the homes, then you probably shouldn't swap out the windows. The reason being, you'd be throwing money at a situation without getting an appraisal that reflects your investment. However, if you're the only house on the street with old windows; that will definitely matter. So again, it's mandatory that you know your area and know your numbers.

Something else to consider with windows as well is how they impact the occupancy inspection. As we've mentioned, where we buy houses, they require a safety inspection, to make sure the house is safe to live in. One of the most important things they inspect is the windows. If the windows cannot be opened, because they've been painted shut or if the wood frames have twisted and swollen, or if they keep falling shut when you open them, these are all big safety issues. What if there's a fire and people can't get out? You need functional windows. Period. But if they are old and functional, and go with the style of the neighborhood, then you can leave them in.

Sometimes we paint windows, however that costs more than you would expect. We had an older house where we thought we were going to save some money by painting the windows. By the time it takes for somebody to carefully put two coats of paint around all the windows, with the different panes, the detail work can be a freaking nightmare. So rather than having somebody paint it, you'll probably be better just replacing it. It could be cheaper, and you're going to have a new window. This is great because tenants love new windows because they're easier to use, and they're more energy efficient, which saves them money on utility bills. And you won't have to worry about replacing them anytime soon.

You're going to want to find a good window company. Call around a lot. Also, a lot of the companies that do a lot of advertising are not going to be the lowest price. They've got to make up for their advertising costs. A good window company is a great addition to your power team. Just keep in mind that certain scenarios call for replacing them, and in other scenarios it's not worth replacing them. Know your numbers, know your neighborhood, and know your ARV.

Inside the House

When we project plan for the inside of the house, we make a note of the bedrooms/bathrooms. Let's say we have a three bed, one bath house. We will walk into the family room and dining room area. There could be old carpeting, an old bronze light fixture, etc. This is an easy one; we're going to rip out the carpeting and replace the light fixture. You can use a notepad, but we use the notes app on our phone, and make a note. "Family room: remove carpeting, replace light fixture." Ninety percent of the time we paint the walls of the house and do something to the flooring. We either sand down and refinish hardwood floors, or we cover them with LVT (luxury vinyl tile). Those are typically the things that are always going to happen. The cost of painting and re-doing floors can add up quickly depending on the size of the home. In this case, the square footage really matters. However, in all reality, those costs can be pretty low in terms of the entire budget.

For hardwood to be sanded and refinished, it currently costs around $2.50 per square foot where we live. Sometimes we install luxury vinyl tile, or the luxury vinyl planks, which is just vinyl flooring that clicks together or peels and sticks. Our preference is the type that clicks together. We also want our vinyl floor to be a little bit more rubber backed, and not the harder vinyl. The harder flooring tends to break and is harder to install. We like the rubber backed ones; they're easier to install, and you can cut that vinyl with an Exacto knife. What's also nice about getting the vinyl flooring is it is "tenant proof" (or shall we say tenant resistant). By that, we mean, if someone drops a glass of wine on the ground, or they drag a fridge across it, they're less likely to scratch or stain the flooring because it's not wood or carpet. It's rubber essentially, it's vinyl. They can still tear it up, but most of those products are guaranteed in residential homes for ten years. That's the lowest guarantee we've seen on them. We've been using this in all our rentals. We like hard surfaces as opposed to carpet, because carpet can get gross. If you get cheap carpet, or even expensive carpet, it's probably only going to last through one or two tenants before you have to replace it. People who rent properties tend to be a little harder on the property than an owner. They seem to care a little less about the condition of the home because it's not theirs. This is okay, you just need to go into it knowing that this is the situation. People tend to treat their own possessions better, that's just the way the world works. The Luxury Vinyl Tile tends to hold up pretty well for multiple tenants or turn overs.

After the flooring and walls, we like to make note of the light fixtures. This is pretty general in terms of the house. It applies to all rooms. We're looking at the big picture here. We look at walls, floors, then light fixtures. Light fixtures are relatively inexpensive, and they make a house look a lot newer and updated by swapping them out. Old light fixtures are hard to clean, they get dirty, and quite often, cleaning them leads to frustration and/or breaking them. That's just been our experience. Rather than cleaning the light fixtures, we'd rather take them out and put new ones in. This also allows you to get all matching finishes from room to room. We like brushed nickel as it is more modern and usually not the most expensive finish like the rubbed bronze or darker black finish. Remember you have to balance cost with price and our personal preferences. In Bedrooms we bite the bullet and install ceiling fans in every bedroom controlled with a wall switch.

All these fixes make the home more welcoming. It's a quick and easy fix with minimal cost to put in a light fixture versus lots of other things involved in the rehabbing process. You get a lot of bang for your buck.

Walls, floors, and light fixtures are pretty generic fixes to a house. Now we'll discuss the more granular modifications like kitchens and bathrooms. So bath and kitchen updates are where you're going to spend a little bit more money. And it's definitely possible to go over budget and overspend in these areas. So you really want to be cognizant of this when rehabbing a property.

Kitchen

With a property that we're rehabbing right now, the cabinets are in pretty good shape but they're old. They've got a really dark stain on them and they have that old brass hardware. The countertops are all dinged up. So with this house, we make notes that say, "replace countertops, paint the cabinets, replace hardware." Appliances can be subjective, depending on the condition. If you have really old, beat up appliances, then you might have to replace some of them.

When putting together a rehab plan it's crucial that it aligns with your ARV or your appraisal. You really don't want to overspend, because you won't be able to get that money back in the refinance. And if you underspend, or don't do a proper rehab, it might not appraise high enough to get your money back. It all comes back to knowing your numbers. Something else to consider in your rehab plan, is how the quality of your rehab affects the amount of rent you can collect. People will pay more for a nicer place, however there are upper limits to that before you get diminishing returns from the work you're doing. New, quality appliances are something that can help you collect more in rent. If you leave your old appliances in there, you might not be able to collect top of the market rent for the property, it'll probably be a little less. However, if you put in some nice stainless-steel appliances. You might be able to collect another $100-150 a month. There's not really a right way or wrong way to do it. That's subjective and comes from experience. We're just suggesting that you be proactive and think about these things when constructing a budget, rather than being reactive. Being reactive will either put you over budget or get less rent. So when you construct your plan, you need to be aware of two things. First, ask yourself, "What is the ultimate goal with this rehab? Am I trying to get my property to appraise at a certain value?" Second, "Are these updates going to make a big enough difference that the extra money spent on the rehab is justified by an increase in market rent?"

We almost never use white appliances, because they just get dirty. Not to mention, we usually paint the cabinets white on our lower end rentals to save money. White cabinets with black appliances "pop" a little bit. They add to the wow factor. We use black appliances, a black countertop, and white cabinets. When we add the brushed nickel handles onto the cabinetry, they really look sharp. Remember you can get cabinet hardware from Amazon that looks like higher end 3- or 5-inch Bars for about 25% of the cost you'd pay at hardware stores. They are hollow, not solid, but look great. Shop around and find the best deals you can.

A mom or anyone that's interested in doing a lot of cooking at home, is going to want the rental with the nice kitchen. Same goes with dishwashers and microwaves. New appliances are also less likely to break than the old ones. Less maintenance is a huge factor in our decision making. You really don't want to get a call that a stove doesn't work anymore. You really don't want to waste $200 sending a repair man out to fix a burner on a ten-year-old electric stove, when you could've bought a new one and have been done with it.

Dishwashers and microwaves are important. Neither of these things are required to get an occupancy permit. However, by providing a dishwasher and a microwave, it's going to increase the value of that home, and more often than not, by quite a bit more than you spent on those appliances. So we typically try to add those two. By having a 4-piece appliance set in all rentals we believe it makes the house more desirable and in turn will increase rent.

One thing we like to leave out or take out is garbage disposals. Garbage disposals are our least favorite appliance in rentals. People overestimate their capacities and clog them up constantly. They're hard to clean. They're dangerous to clean if you don't know what you're doing. They frequently get jammed and break. Tenants call the property manager all the time about them. So it increases our maintenance costs. So now we just remove it completely and tell them to not put any food down the sink, throw it out. It's going to save you a lot of time and money in terms of maintenance down the road if you take them out before you rent the house. The sink can still clog, of course. But using a snake or taking out the bottom of the P trap is an easier fix than messing around with a garbage disposal. Those you can troubleshoot for hours. It is not worth it. It could be a couple of hundred dollars if that appliance needs to be replaced.

The flooring in the kitchen often needs to be replaced. We'll try to slide in that vinyl if it's the same height as the rest of the flooring. We like to use a vinyl peel and stick that you can put grout in. This is what we use in a lot of our bathrooms, it looks like ceramic tile that you can use the grout in between. It's vinyl that peels and sticks though, so it is a little bit cheaper. Groutable peel and stick tile is a godsend for rental properties. It looks nice and it's durable.

Let's talk about the total budget for the kitchen. For our latest project, we didn't buy new cabinets. So we saved most of our money by not replacing the cabinets. All we did was have someone paint them. We spent around 500 bucks rather than a couple thousand. We did replace the countertops with a solid black laminate for around 500 bucks. We reused the sink because it was in good shape. The new faucet was about 100 bucks. Appliances were our big-ticket items in the kitchen on this project. We decided the black fridge was in good shape. However, we shelled out for a new gas stove and a microwave. We had to vent the microwave. We also installed a new dishwasher. With our appliance upgrades, we spent around $2000. That's probably a little high but It's a good habit to overestimate your costs rather than underestimating though.

We had new flooring, light fixtures, new countertops, painted the cabinets, and some new appliances. We spent around $4000 on this kitchen. That's pretty typical. We usually spend around 4K-6K. If we had to replace the fridge and cabinets, it would have been a full rehab, and on the upper end of $6000. Sometimes full kitchen rehabs can cost up to 10K. But that's more typical for a mid-price retail rehab than a rental. We try to keep our kitchen projects in a budget of between 4K-6K.

Again, every project is going to be a little different. Sometimes it will be more, sometimes it will be less. The plumbing fixtures are the sink and faucet. The electrical fixtures are the lighting in the kitchen. Then there's the appliances.

Also, this rental would sell for under $100,000 in the St Louis market. Just so you have an idea of the value of the property we're working with. If it's a bigger/nicer rental you're going to have to spend more, but that should be obvious. If this property was in the $110-150k price range, we'd probably have replaced the cabinets. We'd probably go from black appliances to stainless appliances instead. That's typical in higher priced property, and we'd want to match what's typical for that area.

The reason we'd want to do a nicer rehab in a pricier home is for two reasons. First, we want it to appraise out to where we can get all of our money back. Second, we need to be able to hit a price point in terms of rent. We've got to get the condition of the home to where we know the market will support it. If other houses in the area are renting for X, we ask ourselves "why? Are they nice, are they not nice?" It's all about supply and demand. Nobody is going to pay more for your rental, if they can get something nicer for the same or less money somewhere else.

Bathrooms

Bathroom remodels. We tend to use the vinyl peel and stick tile for bathroom floors. It's really good for bathrooms because it's a small space. We're also not as worried about it getting beat up as much. In the kitchen, people are constantly walking on it, possibly moving furniture or appliances across it. However, in the bathroom, there's not a lot of foot traffic, so it works great and looks great. We've used it for a long time and haven't had any issues with it being torn up or damaged. Right now, we get it from Home Depot for the most part, but you can probably source it from any home improvement/flooring store. Again, this previous rehab, the house is valued at under $100k. This definitely affects the decisions we make on the repairs we make.

For our last project, the tub was in decent shape. The tub was a little bit chipped up, but the tile on the wall around the tub was in decent shape. The tiles were those really old colored tiles. You've probably seen those old green and pink tiles that used to be popular back in the 40's and 50's, you know those tiles that are older than us though. We had really ugly green tile on the walls. We had an older vanity and toilet that's okay. Our plan is to spend a thousand dollars in the bathroom and get it to look like we spent $10k. So what we decided to do was replace the toilet with the higher height and elongated bowl. It's a bit more modern. You might not have realized there's rounded toilets vs elongated bowls. The round ones seem ancient in our opinion. The elongated bowls are newer, nicer, and people like them. They're very handy for us Americans with our big butts.

So we typically replace the toilet and the vanity. It's a pretty cost-effective update and can give you a lot of bang for your buck. New vanities usually cost anywhere from 200 to 500 bucks, and a new toilet is probably less than 200. For a rental grade rehab, we usually spend around $200-250 for the vanity and sink combo. We can get these deals at the big box stores. For this project, we had some guys come in and glaze the tub. Glazing is similar to painting but it's a higher quality finish. It's made for hard to stick to surfaces like fiberglass. Plus, it needs to hold up to the constantly wet conditions of a shower bath. It definitely holds up better and is thicker than paint. It's designed to keep moisture on the outside side of it. Also, you need a professional to do it. We've paid anywhere from $500-1000 to get the job done properly.

Another option is to use bath fitters. It's a completely different process where they come and suction a shell around and over your tub. We personally recommend glazing if you can get away with it. It's great. You don't necessarily need to replace the tub. A lot of these older homes we buy have the old cast iron tubs. If you try to remove one of those, you have to take a sledgehammer and break it into pieces. They're heavy. Plus, you typically run the risk of screwing up the flooring or drywall when you remove one of those. They're a lot of work, and a pain in the ass to remove. So we just leave them. If they're rusted out or have four different colors on them, it's easier and cheaper to just glaze them. Then they look brand new. Not to mention, an iron tub is sturdy. It's not going anywhere. The guys we hire come in, sand them down, glaze them, and they look brand new. The cost can be anywhere from 500 to 1200 bucks. However, the cost of replacing that tub is going to be twice that, at least. Not to mention, if you're going to rip out the tub and replace it, you'll probably need a plumbing permit too.

Something we often talk about in our meetings is how to best manage time. In this case, ripping out and replacing the tub doesn't just cost money. It costs time, and time equals money. Applying for the permit, fixing the floor, and the drywall takes time. Once the drywall is up, you gotta let the mud cure, then sand it, then do another coat and sand it. It's not going to happen in one application. It takes several days to get it back in the right shape. Skip that if you can. If the tub is not destroyed, just glaze it. Let's say it costs $1000 to glaze the whole tub and surround. Then it's around $250 for vanity, $150 for a toilet, plus another $350 for the light and the flooring. Altogether, it's under $2000 and it looks like a brand-new bathroom. That's huge.

That's pretty typical. We spend around $2,000 for a bathroom, $5-6,000 for our kitchen, then everything else, like flooring, painting, light fixtures, and landscaping comes out to around another $5-6000 for the entire house. We try to spend right around $15,000 on our rehabs but budget for $20,000. We do this to get our entrepreneurial credit that the bank offers during the refinance. It also looks and feels like a new house. Not to mention, being proactive about fixing problems means we won't get as many surprises later where we have to call in a handyman. We are looking at the big picture the entire time. Sometimes our rehabs cost $20-25k, if we have to replace windows, HVAC, roof, or other big-ticket items. However, we always shoot to spend at least $15K.

Basements

Basements are pretty prevalent here in St Louis. Basements tend to get this dingy nasty feeling in a lot of older homes. There are spiderwebs, they can be damp, and smell bad. We want to fix that problem. Your basement does not have to be gross. There's a super easy fix, paint everything. Paint is your best friend in a rentable rehab. It can really spruce up a place without doing something that needs a permit. We usually paint the ceilings all black, paint the walls all white, and paint the floor grey. This gives us a nice area for relatively cheap. You can turn a basement that nobody wants to walk down into, into a nice place by cleaning it up. The cobwebs are gone, it's not dirty and dusty anymore, and it looks and smells nice. The paint encapsulates everything.

We don't generally redo basements in terms of putting up walls and drywall. If it does have paneling or drywall in decent condition, we'll leave those and paint them. But we're typically not doing any construction in the basement. If anything, we'll do demolition and removal, and clean it up. If the basement has some paneling knocked out or has some water damage, we just rip it out, it's cheap. No need to replace it. Just like the landscape.

Occasionally we have tenants that do crazy things like partition part of a basement to put a bedroom down there. We don't care. We just want to provide them with the canvas so they can do something with it. More often than not, they use it as a place to store their junk which is fine. If we're just cleaning out stuff, painting, and not doing a ton of demo it'll probably cost us $1500 to $2000 to get a basement looking nice. It helps us get a higher rent and makes it more welcoming. Plus, the appraiser might take notice and bump up the value of the home. It's not livable square footage necessarily, but it's clean. They're going to look at their comps and give you a higher value for that property.

It looks nice, and more importantly, it feels nice. It also ties in with the rest of your house you've just rehabbed rather than looking like a spot you missed. You want to keep it all the same. This is also important when it comes to scaling your business. You want to start having a standard. We use the same paint color in every one of our rentals. We typically use the same products in every rental. It helps with stress and keeping our sanity. If we're doing eight projects and trying to put in a different floor in every project, or different light fixtures; we'd lose our minds trying to keep everything straight. It makes our accounting easier.

Using the same paint makes it easier when a tenant moves out. We don't have to figure out what paint we used, it's always the same paint. Same goes if a tenant scratched up or managed to destroy some of the flooring. We've got a bunch of it in our storage unit already. We can just swap out one piece, or paint one section of the wall if need be. Not only is it convenient, but it's a bit cheaper to buy in bulk. We even use the same appliance supplier as well. After you've bought 40 refrigerators from somebody, they're probably going to give you a discount. There're advantages in doing everything the way we're doing it. We love it.

Adding a Bedroom

We frequently buy two-bedroom, one-bath houses. If there's room for it, it's very inexpensive to throw up one wall. We'll add a door and a closet, and we've created a third bedroom. This is easy if it's a good size house like 1000 square feet. We can usually make something happen with the family room dining room combos. If the dining room is separate, it's even easier to turn into a third bedroom. This is huge; you've added another bedroom which adds value, without having to pay for a costly addition. It also increases your rent. We'll typically get 25% more rent, for spending just a couple of hundred bucks worth of materials! The labor will probably be $1000-1500 to add a wall, a door, a closet. We're not putting electrical in that wall. The room should already have electrical outlets in it somewhere. Another cool thing about doing the conversion with the dining room is they often have a pantry. A pantry can convert into a closet easily. The reason we bring this up is because a bedroom, to legally be classified as a bedroom, has to have three things; it has to have a minimum square footage, a closet, and a window to climb out of in case of a fire. These requirements may vary in different metro areas, but that's what they are in St. Louis.

Recap:

We start on the outside, do a walk around, look at the roof, look at the windows, look at the landscaping, look at the gutters, and look at the A/C unit. We take notes on what needs to be repaired, replaced, or painted. Or if something needs to be cleaned up and removed. Removal rather than replacement is usually the best and cheapest option. For example, if there's an old shed, don't replace it. Just rip it down.

When you walk inside, take note of the condition of the walls, floors, and light fixtures. 75% of the house is walls, floors, and light fixtures. The biggest rooms are typically the bedrooms, and the living and family rooms. Don't overthink it. We usually don't replace baseboards, or deal with little minor things. We stick to the major areas; flooring, walls, and light fixtures. In the kitchen, we usually don't replace the cabinets. We can make them look pretty nice by painting them and changing the hardware. However, we typically do put in new counter tops. They're harder to paint/resurface, so new ones make the kitchen look fresh and clean.

We usually buy decent appliances. It helps in two ways. It helps get the appraisal where we need it, and it helps get a higher rent. We also like to update the light fixtures in the kitchen. We might replace the dishwasher, or add a microwave, and remove the garbage disposal. A garbage disposal is not going to get you anymore in rent, but it will increase your need for maintenance. So we take those out.

In the bathroom we typically redo the flooring. We'll try to leave the tile tub surround if there is one and leave the tub. We just glaze it white. We hire people to do the glazing. They cover it up with a beautiful white glossy finish that makes it look brand new. If you didn't know that we glazed it, you'd swear the bathroom is brand new. It really does look great. We also typically replace the toilet and the vanity. Those costs are relatively cheap. We spend about the same amount on labor to install the toilet and the vanity as we do buying those items.

Last but not least, the basement. We don't build it out. We don't spend a bunch of money down there. We clean it out and paint it. We make it look welcoming for somebody to store their stuff or add a bonus living room down there if they want. We get rid of the cobwebs and hire a painter with a spray gun to spray the ceiling black, the walls white, and the floors grey. It really does make it look nice for cheap. Keep it simple and choose durable.

Action Item: As you're walking through houses, make a note of what fixes you'd do. Keep in mind the cost savings approaches we mentioned in this chapter. Are there any ways you could save a little exlru money by fixing than replacing items? Are there repairs that you might have glossed over, but not realize are more important than you thought before?

"Success doesn't happen, it's planned for." - Anonymous

CHAPTER 13

Project Planning

Here we will discuss some tips for rehabbing rentals. These are tips and tricks that can save you time and money. First, you don't want to do the rehab the same way you would for a retail buyer. There's no reason to spend that kind of money on a property when you can probably get the appraisal you need while spending a lot less.

In the previous chapter we did a walk-through inspection of the house, making notes on what repairs we'd like to make. We also established how we prioritize the repairs we're going to make. It's one thing to know what to do, it's another thing to do what you know. We're lifelong learners, and we work off checklists to make sure things get done. Plans change, and we have to know how to go with the flow. The property walk through of the last chapter is how we take notes on what needs to be repaired. It's easy to compartmentalize outside vs.

inside, or kitchen vs. bathrooms, bedrooms, and basement. However, it's inefficient to work on one room at a time. Now you need to think of the project in phases of what needs to be done first so that other parts of the project fall into place.

Occupancy Inspections

These are a couple examples of Occupancy Inspection forms from Municipalities here in St. Louis. (See Occupancy Inspection Checklist Example 1 and 2 at the end of this chapter)

As mentioned in the Seven Habits of Highly Effective People by Stephen Covey we want to begin with the end in mind here. What is required for occupancy? These are the things that must be done. It would be very difficult to learn the building code in its entirety. However, you can get a general sense of what your local area will require before your first project. You can try to address the big things first and leave a little extra in your budget to repair things that come up later.

When you're doing your rehab, part of the process in BRRRR is getting an occupancy inspection. You need an occupancy inspection done after the rehab, but before you can rent. In St Louis it's required. The goal of occupancy inspections is safety. They don't want people to move into units that aren't fit for human habitation. Especially fire safety. However, we feel the scope of the inspections has gone far beyond just the need for safety, but that is another subject entirely.

One reason we believe is because inspectors are inspecting homes in their own neighborhoods. They are recommending "fixes" that may not even be necessary but they're going to require it. The reason we're bringing up the occupancy inspection is because dealing with inspectors can sometimes be costly. They can delay the whole BRRRR process, because you can't rent the property out until it passes the occupancy inspection. So here's a tip when dealing with inspectors, leave a couple of things for the inspector to find. It's best if they're simple things, like not having batteries in your smoke detector. We recommend you leave some easter eggs so to speak that are left for them to find. Again, the job of the inspector is to make sure the property is fit and safe to live in. If they get there and they don't find anything, they're going to look hard for something. It's human nature, people want to feel that their job is justified. The goal is to keep them from looking too hard for anything wrong with your property. Big fixes can cost more money and add delays. Something like leaving batteries out of a smoke detector is great because it's an easy fix. Leave a couple batteries in your car. The point is, it makes it seem like you're solving problems together. Subconsciously you're working together and don't realize it. Therefore, you're building rapport. You're not creating an enemy, but in this case a teammate. They're thinking, "Not only does this guy care about this property but he's willing to make it right." That inspector is not going to be as picky, because he sees that you care about the neighborhood that he probably lives in.

Project Planning

It's important to know the scope and then the order of the project. You'll have to decide if you're going to be the General Contractor (GC) yourself or hire one. A GC is really just the project manager. They're the person that hires and manages all the subcontractors and helps make sure you're getting all things permitted that need permits. We will discuss whether or not to hire a general contractor in the next chapter.

If you're the project manager, you'll need to have a plan upfront so you and your contractors can get working right away after you close on the property. If you're new to investing, and want to jump straight into buying rental properties, we suggest you bring in somebody else who is an experienced investor, and he rehabs properties to rent all the time. That could be another seasoned investor or a GC that does this for other investors. They'll walk in, and notice things that you might not notice. They'll notice the less than obvious things, like whether an electric panel needs to be replaced, or the plumbing stack has a crack in it. New investors might not notice these problems, but they can cost a lot of money. So when you get a house under contract, it's best to invite a seasoned investor to help you make sure your numbers are correct. We personally believe that wholesaling is the best way to start investing. It's a great tool in your belt, and helps you learn the process. It helps you learn your numbers.

Workflow Checklist

In the last chapter we advised making a list of repairs you plan to make. Now is the time to take your walk-through list and put it in order of how the project should flow. It's all pretty logical when you think about it.

1. Get the property cleaned out. Anything you're going to remove you want to rip that out first. If you're going to replace the cabinets, or the vanity in the bathroom, take that stuff out first. Get it out the way. Don't work around it. It makes it simpler for everybody. Same thing with the flooring. If the carpet is gross, just get it out. You're going to replace it anyways. Now you can see what you're working with. Maybe there's hardwood underneath that you might be able to salvage. Rent a dumpster and make Demo day or weekend. This makes it 10x easier. Now you've got a blank canvas to work with.

2. If you are doing any electrical or plumbing work, do that now. This needs to be done before you start putting in walls or patching. If you wait on this, you might need

to redo your walls if additional holes are made for the plumbing or electrical. This is also a good time to replace windows, HVAC, roof, etc. if those need to be replaced. A lot of the safety issues reflected in the occupancy permit get addressed here too.

3. Drywall repair. Wall construction (maybe we are adding another bedroom!). So you want your painters and finish crew to come and patch all the holes and tape and mud and paint the whole house. It's easier to paint before putting in cabinets and light fixtures to paint around.

4. Figure out your materials and take the necessary measurements. Then put together your plan, go shopping, and buy a bunch of your materials. You should probably already have an idea of what you are going to buy from your prior walk through and notes but double check now that the house is cleared out. It's very common to find out you need things mid project, but it's best to use forethought as best you can.

5. Now is when we are going to put the kitchens and bathrooms back together. We usually put in new

countertops, and paint the cabinets, install new hardware on the cabinets.

6. Then we'll install the new flooring. We do this towards the end of the project to make sure it won't get scuffed up by workers since everything is finished.

7. We do all the final touch ups. We touch up paint, add the base boards, add the light fixtures, install appliances, and maybe do some light landscaping. That's the basics of a rental property rehab, and the order of things you want to do.

Occupancy Inspection Checklist Example 1

CITY OF	APPROVED	NOT APPROVED	REINSPECTION OK	ADDRESS	
OCCUPANCY PERMIT INSPECTION				INSPECTOR	
				DATE	PAGE 1 of 3
EXTERIOR				**PREDICATIONS**	
1 Address Numbers					
2 Driveway		X		Seal Cracks in Driveway / Remove glass surface	
3 Carport Parking Surface					
4 Carport					
5 Roof (Flashing, Shingles, Etc.)					
6 Chimney and Flues					
7 Plumbing Vents					
8 Attic Vents					
9 Roof Trim/ Fascia					
10 Gutters/ Downspouts		X		Install Downspout Elbows to Divert water Away from Foundation	
11 Soffit					
12 Siding/ Trim		X		Clean Areas of House Siding	
13 Foundation					
14 Exhaust Vents					
15 Windows/ Trim		X		Paint Rusting Areas of Exterior Basement Windows	
16 Window Screens					
17 Exterior Doors		X		Install Storm Door Closer (heck n Sm	
18 Hosebib Faucets					
19 Air Cond./ Disconnect					
20 Elec. Outlets/ Fixtures		X		Replace Damage GFCI outlet w/ weatherproof cover	
21 Electrical Wiring					
22 Electrical Service/ Drop					
23 Porches/ Steps					
24 Walks (Public/ Private)		X		Seal Crack in Pr. Jate walk	
25 Patio					
26 Yard (Weeds, Trash, Debris)		X		Dispose of All Leaves/ Sticks/ Debris laying in yards	
27 Fencing					
28 Trees/ Shrubs/ Bushes					
29 Insect Infestation					
30 Rodent Harborage					
31 Decks	NA				
32 Swimming Pools/ Spas					
33 Sheds		X		Scrape & paint peeling Areas of Shed Trim to match	
34 Miscellaneous					
35 Detached Garage					
a Roof (Flashing, Shingles, Etc.)					
b Roof Trim/ Fascia/ Soffit					
c Gutters/ Downspouts					
d Siding/ Trim					
e Walls/ Ceiling/ Floors					
f Windows/ Trim/ Sills					
g Outlets/ Switches/ Fixtures					
h Electrical Wiring					
36					
37					
38					

NOTES: _____

_____

_____

_____

_____

221

CITY OF	APPROVED	NOT APPROVED	REINSPECTION OK	ADDRESS
OCCUPANCY PERMIT INSPECTION				INSPECTOR
				DATE AGE **2** of **3**
INTERIOR				**PREDICATIONS**
36 **Living/ Dining Room**				
a Walls/ Ceiling/ Floor	✓			
b Doors	✓			
c Windows/ Trim/Sills	✓			
d Outlet/ Switches/ Fixtures	✓			
e Fireplace	NA			
37 **Family/ Bonus Room**				
a Walls/Ceiling/Floor				
b Doors				
c Windows/ Trim/Sills				
d Outlet/ Switches/ Fixtures				
e Fireplace				
f				
38 **Hall**				
a Walls/ Ceiling/ Floor	✓			
b Doors	✓			
c Outlet/ Switches/ Fixtures	✓			
d Smoke/ CO Alarms	✓			
39 **Bedroom (Master)**				
a Walls/ Ceiling/ Floor	✓			
b Doors	✓			
c Windows/ Trim/Sills	✓			
d Outlet/ Switches/ Fixtures	✓			
e Smoke Alarm	✓			
f				
40 **Bathroom (Master BR)**				
a Walls/Ceiling/Floor	✓			
b Doors				
c Windows/Trim/Sills		X		make windows operable for ventilation
d Outlet/Switches/Fixtures				
e Exhaust Fan	NA			
f Bath Tub/ Shower	NA			
g Toilet				
h Lavatory	✓			
41 **Bedroom**				
a Walls/Ceiling/Floor	✓			
b Doors	✓			
c Windows/Trim/Sills	✓			
d Outlet/Switches/Fixtures	✓			
e Smoke Alarm	✓			
f				
42 **Bedroom**				
a Walls/Ceiling/Floor	✓			
b Doors	✓			
c Windows/Trim/Sills	✓			
d Outlet/Switches/Fixtures	✓			
e Smoke Alarm	✓			
f				
43 **Bedroom**				
a Walls/Ceiling/Floor				
b Doors				
c Windows/Trim/Sills				
d Outlet/Switches/Fixtures				
e Smoke Alarm				

222

	CITY OF	APPROVED	NOT APPROVED	REINSPECTION OK	**ADDRESS**		
	OCCUPANCY PERMIT INSPECTION				**INSPECTOR**		
					DATE		PAGE 3 of 3
	INTERIOR					**PREDICATIONS**	
44	**Hall Bathroom**						
a	Walls/Ceiling/Floor						
b	Doors						
c	Windows/Trim/Sills						
d	Outlet/Switches/Fixtures						
e	Exhaust Fan						
f	Bath Tub/ Shower		X		Provide/Install Functional Tub Stopper		
g	Toilet				mechanism		
h	Lavatory						
45	**Kitchen**						
a	Walls/Ceiling/Floor						
b	Doors						
c	Windows/Trim/Sills						
d	Outlet/Switches/Fixtures						
e	Exhaust Fan						
f	Cabinets/ Counter Tops						
g	Sink						
h	Garbage Disposal						
i	Electric/ Gas Supply						
j							
46	**Basement**						
a	Walls/Ceiling/Floor						
b	Doors						
c	Windows/Trim/Sills						
d	Outlet/Switches/Fixtures						
e	Stairs/ Handrail						
f	Bathroom	NA					
g	Bathroom Venting	NA					
h	Plumbing Waste/ Soil Stacks						
i	Water/ Drain Lines/ Laundry		X		Repair/Replace Leaking Cold Water		
j	Furnace				Shut off Valve For Kitchen Sink		
k	Water Heater				In Basement		
l	Service Panel/ Sub Panels						
m	Smoke Alarm						
n							
o							
p							
q							
47	**Attached Garage**						
a	Walls/Ceiling/Floor						
b	Doors						
c	Windows/Trim/Sills						
d	Outlet/Switches/Fixtures						
e	Electrical Wiring						
f	Separation Wall						
g							

This is to advise you that in accordance with the Property Maintenance Code of _____ pection of the above-mentioned dwelling unit has been made; we have noted conditions, which must be corrected to bring the property into compliance with the City Ordinances. This application for occupancy permit is invalid after 120 days or with any change in occupancy. Repairs should be completed as soon as possible, but must be completed within 120 days from the initial inspection date, or an approved request for an extension of time is to be obtained. When all repairs are completed, contact the Building Department at _____ schedule a re-inspection. Additional inspections required will result in an additional $50.00 fee for each additional re-inspection. This fee must be paid prior to scheduling any additional re-inspections. If you disagree with one or more of the above predications, you have the right of appeal to the Property Maintenance Board of Appeals within 30 days of the inspection upon written notice to the Building Division. A new owner/ tenant cannot occupy the property without having been issued an occupancy permit or conditional occupancy permit.

INSPECTION REPORT RECEIVED BY _____

Occupancy Inspection Checklist Example 2

CITY OF **OCCUPANCY INSPECTION CHECKLIST**

Planning & Community Development

Address: _____

Contact Name: _____

Phone: _____ Imail: _____

Accepted by: _____

CK# 1574 PD No 0

Permit # _____

Sale: _____ COLLECT

Exterior

P	F	
X	☐	Address/Mailbox _____
X	☐	Roof/Flashing _____
X	☐	Driveway _____
X	☐	Sidewalks _____
X	☐	Garage/Carport _____
☐	☐	Walls _____
☐	☐	Fascia/Soffits/Overhang _____
☐	X	Gutters ELbows/D. Spouts Required w/ Blocks
☐	☐	Windows/Screens _____
☐	☐	Foundation _____
☐	☐	Exterior Doors _____
☐	☐	Deck/Porch/Patio _____
☐	X	Lighting Rear lights MISSing BULbS
X	☐	Electric Service Line _____
☐	X	GFCI Receptacles Rear Recep GFCI Required
☐	☐	Accessory Structure _____
X	☐	Yard/Pool/Fence _____

Interior

X	☐	Kitchen walls, floors, ceiling _____
X	☐	Outlets, fixtures _____
X	☐	Exhaust fan, stove _____
X	☐	GFCI _____
X	☐	Cabinets _____
X	☐	Dining Room walls, floors, ceiling _____
X	☐	Outlets, fixtures _____
☐	☐	Fireplace _____
X	☐	Living room walls, floors, ceilings _____
X	☐	Outlets, fixtures _____
☐	☐	Fireplace _____
X	☐	Hall walls, floors, ceilings _____
X	☐	Outlets, fixtures _____
X	☐	Carbon Monoxide Detector _____
X	☐	Hall Smoke Detector _____
X	☐	Hall Bath walls, floors, ceilings _____

P	F	
X	☐	GFCI, outlets, fixtures _____
X	☐	Tub, shower, toilet, shut offs _____
☐	☐	Hall Bath 2 walls, floors, ceilings _____
☐	☐	GFCI, outlets, fixtures _____
☐	☐	Tub, shower toilet, shut offs _____
X	☐	Laundry walls, floors, ceiling _____
X	☐	GFCI, fixtures _____
X	X	Dryer Vent Required in Laundry to Exterior
X	☐	Master Bed walls, floors, ceilings _____
X	☐	Outlets, fixtures _____
X	☐	Smoke detector _____
X	☐	Master Bath walls, Floors, Ceilings _____
X	☐	GFCI, outlets, fixtures _____
X	☐	Tub, shower toilet, shut offs _____
X	☐	Bed 2 walls, floors, ceilings _____
X	☐	Outlets, fixtures _____
X	☐	Smoke detector _____
X	☐	Bed 3 walls, floors, ceilings _____
X	☐	Outlets, fixtures _____
X	☐	Smoke detector _____
☐	☐	Bed 4 walls, floors, ceilings _____
☐	☐	Outlets, fixtures _____
X	☐	Smoke detector _____
X	☐	Basement finished room _____
X	☐	Basement unfinished room _____
X	☐	Basement Bath _____
X	☐	Water Heater _____
X	☐	Furnace _____
X	☐	Electric Panel _____
X	☐	Utilities _____
☐	☐	Room Sizes 12x11, 13x12, 12x12
☐	☐	Room Sizes _____
☐	☐	Additional Notes _____
☐	X	Stairways HANDRail Rear floor steps

☒ **MUST BE RE-INSPECTED**
☐ **APPROVED FOR OCCUPANCY**

Ok to issue: _____

DATE: _____

Of Bedrooms ___3___

INSPECTOR: _____

INSPECTOR: _____

Occupancy Load ___7___

224

Recap:

1. **Occupancy Inspections:** These are a priority. Without passing the occupancy inspection, we can't rent out the property. These fixes don't always make objective sense in our opinion. However, it's best to work as a team with them for the safety of your tenants.

2. **Project Planning:** If you're new to the rehabbing process, consult with other investors or contractors for help. It's easy to overlook expensive issues until you get experience.

3. **Workflow Checklist:** We walk through the house, going room by room to make notes on necessary repairs. However, construction happens in phases, in a particular order throughout the house.

Action item: In the last chapter you made a list of what repairs you would need to make on a property. Let's take that list and restructure it, so work flows smoothly from one phase to the next.

"Workflow and usability are not afterthoughts; they impact the core of any project and dictate how it should be engineered." -Ryan Holmes

CHAPTER 14

Hire A General Contractor or Do It Yourself?

The next topic is whether or not you should be the General Contractor (GC) on this project or if you want to hire a GC. There is no right or wrong answer with this. Both ways work great, but there are obviously advantages and disadvantages to both of these strategies. Mike is usually the GC on a lot of our projects. He's also working with other general contractors to help speed up.

Here are some things to consider when deciding on which strategy is better for you. If you've never swung a hammer before that's okay, you can GC a job. If you don't like painting or any manual labor, you can still be the GC. The GC is just the general contractor, or basically the project manager. You're the owner of the property, and you're telling people what to do. You come up with a plan for the property. You walk through each room. You make decisions on what needs to happen where and when. Then you figure out who is going to do each of those items for you.

You're most likely going to have to pick out the materials and deliver them. Although, this depends on your contractors and what they're willing and able to do for you.

Hiring a GC comes with a couple of advantages. First off, you have an expert at managing projects. He should have a bunch of subcontractors that can work for him for even less than you'd be able to hire them for. It's hands off for you, but they obviously want their cut. In exchange, it's going to cost you more. You're paying a person to manage other people for you as well as share their experience. As mentioned previously a GC can come and look at a property with you when you are under contract and give their insight into the cost of rehab and what to do.

You can save money by trying to be the GC for a project yourself. You can learn a lot of lessons. However, you can lose a lot of money by doing it yourself too if you don't know what you're doing. For example, you might have somebody come in and do the floors. Then realize you should've painted first. If your painters are messy, they could mess up your carpet or your new floors. So not doing repairs in the right order can have consequences. It's a process and a learning curve. But if you know what you're doing, or you've made a couple mistakes and learned from it, that's ok. That's how we both learned. We've made every mistake in the book, but that's why we're doing well today. If you learn it and do it yourself, it's typically going to be cheaper.

When you hire a GC, you may pay a little bit more, but it's very hands off. When we hire a GC, we only have to go to the property three times. We go once when we buy it, once when we meet our GC to show them the work that we need to do and get a quote. Lastly, we go to review the work that was done, and make sure it meets our standards of quality. If everything looks good, he is done, and we pay him. This is only after we have done several projects together and trust that they are doing quality work. On the first few projects we want to stop by a few times a week to monitor what they are doing. It would be a good idea to go and see what is happening to your property to learn as well. Seeing all the work that goes into a job is exciting. It feels great to see progress. You might also learn that some things aren't as hard as you thought. Or you might develop a new respect for the work that is done.

When you're hiring a GC, you're not managing the people anymore. Instead you're now managing your general contractor. The advantage here is that it's way more hands off for you. You're not having to interview people to do these particular jobs. You're most likely not even buying the materials for these jobs. You're hiring somebody else to step in and do that. Most GC's have their own sub-contractors they use. They have carpenters, electricians, plumbers, you name it. That can really speed up the project. However, when you hire a GC, you're generally going to be paying a bit more for that project.

However, if you hire right, you should get a lot of added value in return. Just like when we buy a property from a motivated seller off market. We're providing them convenience at a low cost. All we're doing when we hire a GC is trade money for them to provide us with convenience.

They're stepping in to manage the project. They're going to be taking all the calls, dealing with the inspectors, buying materials and dealing with the sub-contractors. That's all their problems now. But obviously, that convenience comes at a cost. There are pros and cons to both sides. There is really no right or wrong way to do it. It just depends on how active you want to be in that part of the business. How fast do you want to scale? It's very difficult to scale if you're the GC for eight projects or more while you're also trying to acquire new ones. It's even harder if you're not only the GC but you're also doing the work yourself. Doing the work, yourself is going to slow you down even more.

Something to consider when making the decision to hire a GC or not is your stress tolerance. How much of your time and energy do you want to spend on this project? If you have a lot of free time, then maybe GC'ing makes sense for you. However, if you work a full-time job like many of our students, you might not want to take on the stress. Are you willing to pay a little more to hire one manager versus orchestrating all the moving parts? How well you handle stress and/or time is a big factor when making the decision of hiring a GC. This also applies to scaling your business, or if you're working multiple deals at once. If you're like us, and want to maximize the BRRRR strategy, you have to buy a bunch of properties at once in order to scale your business. If that's the case, you can't be doing plumbing work or other odd tasks. You'll become the bottleneck. At that point you have to start hiring GC's, because you can't be in multiple places at the same time. You have to work with people you can count on and trust to manage your projects. That's an issue with scaling. If you're doing it all yourself, scaling may not even be an option, or it is going to be very difficult. If you're hiring people, you have to develop a sense of trust and communication to make sure the jobs are done right when you're not there.

The next set of pros and cons to consider is liability. You may hire a GC who has liability insurance. All of those subs are going to essentially be covered with workman's comp, or just in case of an injury. If you're doing it yourself, you may not have all those same insurance policies.

Earlier we had mentioned paying your sub-contractors. If you're providing materials, then you may have to pay that individual via a W2. However, if they're providing the materials, you may be able to pay them with a check and issue a 1099 at year end. This may or may not help you with taxes. We can't tell you which way is right because it all depends on your unique situation. There's no right answer to that question. Talk to your local accountant or CPA and figure out what makes the most sense to you. All of which circle back to knowing your numbers and doing what's right for your current situation.

Finally, you need to put something in writing with your GC. Once you've selected a GC you want to work with you need to put in writing what the expectations are from each party. This is not difficult, just identify who is paying for what, who is doing what, and when payment will be made. I put together a 1-2-page scope for each project that the GC and myself sign every time even after we have done multiple projects together.

For more information, check out our online course www.FreeLandlordCourse.com.

Three Variables

Something we always keep in mind when starting a new project is our expectation on time, quality, and cost. Those are your three variables. How long is it going to take? How much is it going to cost? And what is the quality of the rehab? In general, this goes for all rehabbing or any project in general. Time, quality, and cost are your key variables. When you're dealing with a general contractor, you can typically pick two of those three. There are tradeoffs that you need to be willing to make. Are you willing to sacrifice quality to keep the project fast and cheap? If you want to keep costs down and quality high, then your project is definitely going to take longer. Lastly if you want high quality work delivered in a short period of time, you're going to pay a lot more. It's as simple as that.

You just need to evaluate your priorities and pick two of those three. The reality is, you can't have all three. You're never going to find it. Keep that in mind when you are GC'ing the project, or if you hire a GC for that project. Pick two of the three and expect the other one to suffer. If it doesn't, that's a bonus.

This is important because there can be a huge variance in cost. We've gotten bids on kitchens that have had a variance in cost of $10k. That's insane. One thing we will always ask is, "What's the cost? How long is this going to take? What quality of work are you giving me?" Quite often, the bid doesn't align with our goals and objectives. For the BRRRR method, the rehabs we're doing is for rental properties. We can sacrifice quality a little bit. We do not use crystal chandeliers in the kitchen, or travertine tile in the bathrooms. They need to be nice. They need to be comforting and welcoming. We want to attract a tenant. But we don't need to have marble countertops to do that, if that makes sense.

You definitely want to look at those three variables on every job; time, cost, and quality. So get multiple bids and make sure your bids align with your goal and your plan.

Those variables are super important, because it all circles back to knowing your numbers.

How to Pay Your Contractors

You can pay your contractors one of two ways. You can have them give you a fixed bid like $500 to paint all the cabinets, etc. A lot of times a fixed bid is the best way to go. The other option is to pay hourly. If you're paying hourly and they're working slow, then it's going to cost you more than if you do a fixed bid. When it's a fixed bid, it incentivizes them to speed up, because then their hourly wage is increased if they are working less hours.

There are pros and cons to each. With fixed bids, they're generally going to work a little faster, but they may cut corners. You might have to double check or triple check the work to make sure that it's done properly before you write that final check. With a fixed bid, a lot of sub-contractors are going to ask for half the money up front, then the other half upon completion. This is probably not your friend; this is more of a business relationship. We never pay anyone, the full amount before the project is COMPLETE. We'll repeat that again for emphasis. NEVER PAY ANYONE THE FULL AMOUNT BEFORE THE JOB IS DONE. You absolutely cannot do that. Every time I've heard of an investor getting burned by a contractor, that's how it happened. They always paid too much in the beginning, the contractor flaked out, and there is no recourse for that individual. We typically try to avoid even paying half down up front. We've found it best to buy materials, and give them a few days' pay, or a small amount of money to get started. We've found that paying in thirds is often better than paying half up front, and half on the back end. This means paying a third to start the project, a third upon an established milestone, and another third upon completion of the project. Find a pay schedule that works for you, but make sure you protect yourself from paying too much money up front before a project is finished.

So again, with fixed bids versus paying contractors by the hour, there are pros and cons to each. How you choose to pay them plays a factor in the three variables we just discussed. You need to interview these people before you hire someone.

If someone says they've done this kind of work before, you need to ask for samples of their projects. The proof is in the pudding. We live in the "Show Me State". If we can, we'd like to go out and look at their projects. Another option is to check their Facebook page for their before and after photos of projects. Do they have a website? You can check that too. Or you can ask for references. You also want to get multiple bids. This is important. Don't let just one person go out to your job site and give you a bid without getting bids from other contractors. And don't feel guilty that you can't hire everyone. This is their job. They look at different job sites and get bids. It's pretty standard to get three bids or more.

How you pay the contractors might depend on who is buying materials, and we do it a lot of different ways. On buying materials, the IRS is pretty strict on that. If you are buying the materials, and you are paying that person, they might be considered an employee. So you want to be careful with that. Talk to your accountant and plan ahead. Everybody will have a different strategy and that's okay. Some of that stuff is kind of a grey area on what you want to do. Even if it's pretty black and white, you should get their opinion, and do it the right way. That is what we recommend.

Hiring Subcontractors

Each situation is going to have a different solution. We'll discuss how we hire a GC, or subcontractors. If you're new to this, you're going to want to hire some subcontractors or laborers to help you with these projects, unless you want to do the work yourself. In that case, you would be the subcontractor or laborer yourself. But if you are GC'ing the project yourself, then you'll need to hire people to do these jobs. Depending on what is needed, some laborers are great at a lot of things. They can lay flooring, paint, hang drywall, and do minor carpentry work. However, certain projects require more specialized workers. You might need to find yourself a carpenter for certain projects. The first place we recommend for finding subcontractors is simply tapping into your personal network. You can do this by going on Facebook or your local REIA. Don't go to a nationwide group with 50,000 people. That's too overwhelming. Find one that has anywhere from 500-5000 people in it at most. Most of these groups have people promoting handyman work. They don't specialize in anything in particular, but they can do a lot of little different things. Find these people and interview them. You want to get a lot of bids and estimates.

You can post on your Facebook that you bought a house and you need help with it. You might have a friend, or a friend of a friend who is out of work. They could be willing to work with you at a good price. It's a win-win.

By the time you hire a handyman, you should hopefully have your game plan in order, and have a budget. You have to work those things out in advance. Then you can purchase the materials. Ideally, you want to be the project manager not the project worker.

As we suggested earlier; post on Facebook, or look at the local handyman group and say, "I have a rental property, and I need someone to do this...." You should be able to find the person you need. Something to consider is if the work needs a permit. You may or may not know at this point in time. A lot of the stuff is just going to be learned along the way. That's okay, take action.

For example, if there is a little leak in the shower, you might just need to replace the knobs on the shower valves. Replacing those doesn't require a permit, it's easy. A plumber would know that and be able to fix that for you. If you buy a house that has structural issues, you may need an engineer to come up with a construction plan and obtain a permit. If you don't know, talk to the county or the city about whether or not you need a permit. It's such an asset to know and hire the right people. If you're wondering why anyone would even buy a house that has structural issues, it's because you can get a really good deal on it! We love huge discounts!

How to Manage Subcontractors

If you're going to GC this project, you have to be good at managing people and cost. If you're not good at that, or you have no interest in that; then GC'ing the project yourself might not be a good idea. You may want to hire one, which we are going to get too soon. Ask yourself, "Am I a people person? Am I good at managing people?" That's definitely something to keep in mind when making the decision about hiring a GC or being the GC yourself. Anytime we hire a contractor, we know it doesn't always work out in a beautiful situation where everybody wins. Dealing with contractors can be difficult. The idea is to make it a win-win for both you and them. You want to build a relationship to where you can work with them in the future. You'll get better pricing and build trust.

However, that doesn't always happen. We hire a lot of people that we may only hire one time. The only way to find and meet those good contractors is to work with a lot of them. Don't be discouraged if you hire somebody and it doesn't work out exactly the way you envisioned it. There was probably an issue with your communication, or maybe something on their end that you had no control over. It happens. We still hire people to this day that we have to fire. When this happens, we simply say, "It was nice working with you. We appreciate you doing work for us on this particular job." It can take time, however, by doing this over and over, we've found people that are reliable, and do great work. They want to keep working for you and you want to keep hiring them. There can be a lot of trial and error that goes into that process, especially in the beginning. Just know that it's okay, it's natural, it's normal, and it's all a part of the learning process. Everybody is dealing with that same issue.

Let's say you're dealing with subcontractors. You have to determine whether you want to be managing people as well as cost. You need to determine who is going to be buying those materials.

Managing the Project

We like to be the early birds and get out to the projects before most of the crew shows up. We'll take pictures and inspect the house. Then when the GC calls up and has a question, we have an idea of what's going on. It's not spying or anything, it's our project, we own the house and everything in it, except any tools they left behind. We're paying them. So we can check in on their work any time we want. It keeps them honest. It's very insightful to know how they maintain their project site. We like to know if they have materials scattered everywhere, or if they didn't sweep up at the end of the day. It's an indication of how they operate. If it's a messy work site, it gives off a bad impression. A sloppy work site could mean sloppy work. How people do anything is how they do everything. A messy work site creates more room for errors, losing things, for messing things up. Also, it's going to slow the project down. In this business, time equals money. It could also be dangerous in some situations.

If somebody comes in with a big heavy tub, or other big heavy equipment, you don't want them walking around with nails and staples on the ground.

"If it's a messy work site, it gives off a bad impression. A sloppy work site could mean sloppy work."

They're going to grind that stuff into the floor or open themselves up to injuring themselves or damaging the property. Not taking care of the property when they are there is a red flag for us. We'll probably consider somebody else next time unless we can mitigate the problem.

If we encounter a sloppy work site, we like to work with the GC on fixing that problem. We ask, "What's going on? How come the house is so dirty? They might reply with the excuse that they're rehabbing the house, and that's just the way it is.

If so, you can suggest that they clean up at the end of the day, to make it a better working environment. You may or may not even want to have that conversation. Habits can be hard to break. You might just decide to work with someone else next time; someone who takes pride in their project and takes pride in their work. The little things make a huge difference in our opinion. Sometimes it's worth that little bit extra. The devil is in the details.

Scaling

We think it's best to prepare for scaling. With that said though, even if you're not doing the work yourself, you still need to check in on the property every couple of days, probably every day. You should be going out to the property and checking to make sure the work is being done properly and in a timely manner. You're still managing the GC when you hire them. You're just not managing all the other things. By hiring a GC you've simplified the process.

Recap:

1. **Hiring A GC vs. Being The GC:** General Contractor just means project manager. Do you want to manage the project and subcontractors or somebody else? There's no right or wrong way. Both have pros and cons, and you'll learn from both methods.

2. **Three Variables:** The three variables are price, quality, and time. You can pick your two of the three to line up with your priorities.

3. **How to Pay Your Contractors:** Never pay all the money up front! You can pay some money up front or for completion of different milestones. However, you need to protect yourself by only paying the full amount upon satisfactory completion.

4. **Hiring Subcontractors:** A great way to find subcontractors is to reach out to your network. Ask around on social media or a local REIA.

5. **How to Manage Subcontractors:** Managing contractors is all about communication and setting clear cut expectations up front.

6. **Managing the Project:** Until you develop a strong relationship built on trust, it's best to inspect the job site frequently to check on the quality of work. A sloppy work site could mean sloppy work or other problems.

7. **Scaling:** You can only be in one place at one time. To grow your company, you'll eventually have to get comfortable hiring GC's, even if you like that work.

Action Item: If you need a GC or subcontractor, make a post to social media or find one at your local REIA. Discuss with them your goals and objectives. This includes price, time, and quality. When you get bids, make sure you have the scope of work and expectations in writing before hiring or paying anyone.

"Communication is the bridge between confusion and clarity." -Nat Turner

CHAPTER 15

Rehabbing Case Studies

S tory time with Mike: Before I was full time, I'll be honest, I don't even remember the cost, the numbers, or anything like that. I purchased a four-family unit back in 2009. I purchased if off the MLS. It was kind of run down, but it was in a decent area. Three of the units were rented and one was vacant. So, I was going to move into it myself. I did literally everything wrong. I rehabbed it like I was going to live there, because I was living there. I got new cabinets in the kitchen. I made it nice. That one still gets me a little bit more rent because it has that dishwasher and features that the other ones don't. But anyways, I did most of the GC and work myself. I had never done any of that type of work before. I painted it. I put the base boards up. I bought an air compressor, all that stuff. I also hired a buddy who was an electrician by trade, he helped me with some of the other stuff. In any case, I was way over budget for sure, but it was a good learning experience. It was fun. I think a lot of us real estate investors got our start by doing a lot of the project planning and work ourselves. It just becomes a part of your journey, and there is no better way to learn than doing the projects yourself and being hands on in the beginning. I do think it is worthwhile. Even though I have no desire to do it anymore.

Story Time with Dave: So, when I first started real estate investing full time, I bought a house for $19,000 and I put $25,000 in it. It's kind of crazy because I didn't have much labor cost, because I was the main laborer. The project took seven months. Seven months for one rehab seems crazy now. We've done over 100 rental rehabs now and our average takes around 2 months. It's okay, you get better the more you do it. So, don't stress out if your first rehab takes you six months. It's not a big deal. Even if they all take six months, you can do one or two a year and keep adding rental properties to your portfolio every year. That's huge.

I learned a lot from that seven-month rehab. I learned what exactly needs to be done. In this particular house everything needed to be done. It felt like a curse because I spent seven months working on it. Looking back on it though, it was actually a blessing. I learned how to do plumbing, minor electrical work, hang drywall, lay tile, install cabinets, etc. I even put on a countertop. Before then, I had never even swapped out a vanity or a toilet. There were so many things I had to learn on this project. I had to hire someone to do the roof, but I was right there with them, helping them.

This was such an important learning experience, because now when I walk through a property, I know immediately what's ok and what won't fly. I instinctively know if the inspector is going to red flag it, or if I need to fix something to get higher rent. Learning is a process that comes from experience.

When you actually do the work on a project, you realize how much work each one of those jobs is. You know what all it entails to get the job done right. Or, you recognize that some things aren't as difficult as you would've thought.

It's not uncommon for us to meet new investors who don't really have an understanding of repair costs. We just met a guy that we were trying to help out. However, he was new to the game and had an unreasonable expectation on repair costs. He just didn't have the experience yet. He was buying houses at a tax auction. These houses had been abandoned for five to six years. He was buying them for about $10-25,000. These houses needed around $50k worth of work. He didn't know though. He assumed they could be done for around $15-20k. However, we estimated repairs to be around $40-50 per foot. He didn't know his numbers as well as we do. He's going to learn almost everything he needs to know on just this one project. Any money he loses, is going to get paid back ten-fold with experience. It's going to help him with every project beyond that.

We're coaches. We're not trying to be mean or difficult. We don't want to tell people their wrong, but we're trying to give our guidance to save people money and headaches. Our advice was to double his budget. Then if you come in under budget, you've done fantastic. However, if you have an expectation of low rehab costs, and you blow your budget, you're going to feel like it's a huge failure. You have to embrace the whole process as a learning experience. You're paying for real world education too.

The great thing is he's out there doing it. So good for him, I hope he keeps it up. Hopefully we didn't come off too mean, we're actually proud of him. 99% of people would rather sit around and watch 15 more episodes of something on TV, and never do anything. The fact that he's jumping in and doing it is giving him a huge leg up. He probably won't make any money on that deal, but the experience he gains will set him up for future success.

When we both started, we did a lot of the work ourselves. We did it from the perspective of being the GC. We were the ones dealing with and hiring subcontractors. So, when we bought a rental, we'd come up with a game plan. We'd walk through each room and make decisions on what to keep, fix, or replace. Does the tub look bad, are cracks in the tile, is the vanity leaking? There are so many decisions to make. Many fixes like plumbing or electrical work are beyond our capabilities. We needed to find somebody who knows better than us in those areas. If you keep at this, and treat it all as a learning experience, you will get better and more confident. We're living proof.

"There can be no learning without action, and no action without learning." -Reg Revans

PART IV

RENTING

CHAPTER 16

Showing the Property

The section of the book is about renting the property out. We'll discuss advertising, the property, showing the property, and tenant screening. We'll tell you about things to watch out for when renting a property. We'll also give tips on rent collection, how leases work, and how to manage a property. We'll also talk about the pros and cons of hiring a property manager.

Preparing the Property for Showing

There are so many things to learn and understand. Our goal is to keep it simple. Let's say we've already bought and rehabbed a property, and now we're ready to rent. To do this we need to make sure the rehab has been completely finished. That means all the tools and materials are out of the house. Everything has been cleaned and prepped. The rehab is not complete until prospective tenants can walk through it. The last thing they want to see are tools strewn about, or a dirty and dusty house. That stuff needs to be done before you invite people in. So make sure the rehab project is absolutely complete. Then you can focus on renting it. Don't try to blur those lines. That's very important. We're also not a fan of letting the neighbors walk through until the property is finished. Tell them they are welcome to come back later to check it out when you are finished. Until then, think of it as a construction site. unless it is pretty well cleaned up. You don't want them to get hurt.

This can be a confusing point for us mentally. In St Louis we have to get occupancy inspections in almost all of our municipalities. When the occupancy inspection happens, an inspector comes in and looks around the property to make sure it's safe and up to code; whatever their codes are for the property. We get the place fixed up and cleaned out. We need to pass the occupancy inspection prior to getting a tenant in place. That can affect our timeline. We often wonder what we should do first. Should we clean it first? Should we have the property manager try and rent it first? We usually clean it first. Ideally, we want to clean it right before we show it, but the occupancy inspection needs to come after the repairs. The cleaning and inspection can overlap, but we want to make sure we get all these things done in a timely manner. Time is of the essence is our point. If you stretch this process out to six or eight months, the BRRRR strategy is worth less. Time costs money. REAL MONEY. You have holding costs like taxes and insurance at the minimum, as well as the cost of interest on the money you borrowed or used to rehab. There are also vacancy costs. We look at all of our projects as vacant properties because they are vacant. When we think about a vacant rental, we know that is lost revenue. The longer a house is vacant, the longer you are not collecting rental income on it and your costs are adding up. Speed it up!

Once your rehab is nearing completion, make sure you are contacting the city, or municipality that does the inspection. Make sure you've got your ducks in a row and set up, because sometimes they can be on a several week backlog. Not to mention, whenever we get the occupancy inspection scheduled, they almost always find something that needs to be repaired. Sometimes it's minor, but sometimes it's major. That can really slow things down even more. We try to get that going right away. When we're near the finish line on a project we bring in our cleaners, and get the inspection scheduled. Maybe it doesn't matter, but we think having a clean house that's just rehabbed helps us with the inspection. Having a clean property reflects a sense of attention to detail. So hopefully they'll take it easy on us. We're trying to make the property a nice place to live, which is why there's inspections in the first place. We're not slumlords. This is huge.

After the property is cleaned, and the occupancy inspection is done, we like to start showing it right away. Time is money. There's a couple of options. We can hire somebody to show it and do the leasing, or we can do the showing and application process ourselves. Either way, we want to start collecting applications. With our property looking very appealing, we should get a lot of people who want our product. We should get a lot of applications. We'd rather turn away a lot of people than have to pick somebody we don't want to rent to. Having a lot of well qualified people is a good problem to have. As applications come in, then we go through the process of screening the tenants.

Advertising the Property

Before we can show the property to prospective tenants, we need to advertise our property. One of the easiest ways we've found to entice prospective tenants is putting a sign in the yard. It's super easy, and only costs a couple dollars to get a sign at a hardware store. People driving by in the subdivision are generally speaking located fairly close. They're not some random person moving from across the country that doesn't have a sense of the area. They're usually somebody moving from one house to another, in the same neighborhood or same city. They could be a friend/family member that lives in that neighborhood and want their loved ones to live closer to them. People driving through the neighborhood are going to see that sign and call on it. This is a powerful, and often overlooked tool. We also do this with our wholesale/rehab business. We put 'We buy houses' signs outside, and near our rehab projects, on every project. People see us working on a house and they get excited or interested. It's a great lead source.

The second big way we advertise rental property is online. We use the free tools out there to get our property advertised. It costs us nothing which is awesome. Zillow is an amazingly powerful tool. In fact, that's probably the most powerful tool for rentals. We also utilize the Facebook marketplace. There are tons of local Facebook groups where you could make a post about your rental property. "Buy, trade, and sell" groups are great, but you'll probably have to do a little digging to find the right groups for you. There's so many of them. Every market has something different. There's big groups and small groups. We also use Craigslist to advertise our rental property. All of these tools are great. They're free and easy to use. Zillow is great because it syndicates. This means it pushes your info out to other websites automatically.

You shouldn't need any more than that to pull in prospective tenants. If you don't get results from the above suggestions, something else is wrong. Either the condition or price is off for that neighborhood. Having quality pictures helps too. If your property is priced appropriately, you should be able to get it rented on one of those sites or methods.

There are also a couple useful tools for determining a target rent. We mentioned Zillow for advertising, but it's also very helpful for determining rent estimates. Other properties in your area will be posted. Look for similar

"It's a good habit to put yourself in someone else's shoes. Pretend you are a prospective tenant and looking for a house to rent."

properties. Look at their pictures, look at what they're charging in rent. This will help us figure out how much we should be charging for rent. Another great resource is called RentOMeter.com. It's so easy to use, we type in the property address, the bed and bath count, and next pops up what it estimates the rent should be in that area for a similar property. They're pretty accurate too.

It's a good habit to put yourself in someone else's shoes. Pretend you are a prospective tenant and looking for a house to rent. Does this house look nice? Is it competitively priced compared to other houses in the area? What is the competition charging? How does this property stack up? If we have a freshly rehabbed property, someone down the street is probably renting a very similar property. We factor in whether it was the same builder, or the same construction type. Is that house 10 or 20 years outdated? If they're charging $1200, we could probably charge $1400 for ours because we have brand new appliances, nice kitchen cabinets, new flooring, new paint, and it just plain looks nice. Having a nice property means we can probably charge a little bit more, but we have to keep it within reason. That's why it's so important to check out what the competition is doing.

Landlords often get a bum rap as being 'Slumlords'. We try not to be in that category. We really believe that people are choosing to be renters and tenants from us because we offer a better product. We drive by our properties twice a year. Once we just drive by and inspect the interior for issues. Then we repair or help tenants repair items if needed. We want to maintain our properties and help our tenants maintain them. We expect our tenants to pay rent on time and in return they should be able to live in a well-maintained home. It should feel like the day they moved in. We are very responsive to service our tenants. This is not something everyone has the ability to do. Many homeowners don't know where to get started when a furnace or AC unit goes out. We have a relationship with several vendors and can often get an HVAC tech out the same day. That does have a cost to us and of course like all businesses we pass that along to our customer (the tenant). Our knowledge, experience, vendor database, and access to capital for quick and proper repairs is why people rent from us as opposed to renting somewhere else or owning a home.

Showing the Property

We like to set up a showing day. Once we've advertised the property, people call in and ask when they can see it. We like to set up three or four people on the same day. We tell them when we can meet. If they can meet, then great, if not, we just say we'll have to meet the next time. When we go over there, we bring flyers. It's really important to get everybody in there at once. It creates a sense of urgency, and that the property is in demand. Not to mention, it keeps it quick for us, rather than having us running over to the property a bunch of times.

We do a good job on our rentals. They are freshly rehabbed houses, most tenants don't always get to move into a nice, fresh house. Somebody who is renting, often can't buy a house, especially a new house. Having a freshly rehabbed house is pretty cool. We can charge a little bit more rent. We like to put out a desirable product for our tenants. By having a nicer house than the other outdated rentals in the area, we rarely have issues finding tenants or commanding top of the market rent.

When we lease the property, we make it clear what the rent is and what charges are in addition to rent. We charge back for some of the utilities that we pay for on behalf of the tenant. These are Trash and Sewer. We add an additional $75 for these on top of the monthly rent. We have the trash in our name because we do not want any of our properties to go without trash service. The sewer bill has to be in our name because our sewer provider attaches liens to properties if that bill goes unpaid. We just impose a flat rate add on to rent for these items. Tenants can be concerned about this considering we're already getting top of the market rent. It's six one way and half a dozen the other. They're either paying us, or they're paying the utilities directly. We do it this way to protect our interests. Rarely do we get any issue. However, if we do get push back, that's fine. We can rent to the next candidate. Pro tip, if people are a pain in the beginning, they'll be a pain in the end. We have a freshly rehabbed and updated home; it sells itself to the tenants. We do not want to push anyone into one of our properties, especially if they are on the fence if they can afford the rent.

We have several goals when showing the property. We're trying to consolidate our showings to funnel several potential tenants at once. We also want to screen the people that are interested in putting in an application. When tenants ask about applying, that's a great time to discuss the roles and expectations of the tenant and landlord. If you are managing the property yourself, you are going to have an ongoing relationship with the tenant. You're not looking for a friend, but you are looking for someone that seems like a reasonable person. This might be one of the few times you will interact with them prior to renting your property to them. Make the most of it. We always recommend using a service to run a credit and background check as part of your formal application. Zillow Rental Manager and Cozy.Co are two places that you can find these. These checks rarely ever come back perfect, so choose the best one. Also, it gives you a reason for not renting to someone if you don't think they'd be a good fit. Rather than just relying on your gut, you now have data and reports that indicate if someone would be a good renter. We want to make this clear, you have to play by the rules. The Equal Opportunity Housing act makes it illegal for any discrimination in the sale, lease, or rental of housing; or making housing otherwise unavailable because of race, color, religion, sex, handicap, familial status, or national origin. We would never condone acting otherwise. It's illegal, ethically wrong, and doesn't make much business sense to exclude a qualified possible tenant.

Recap:

1. **Preparing the Property for Showing:** Before showing the property, the rehab has to be completely finished. All construction tools need to be taken off site, and the house cleaned. Not only does the property show better, but this is also a safety issue.

2. **Advertising the Property:** There are a ton of ways to advertise your property online. Facebook has "buy, sell, trade" groups. Zillow automatically pushes your rental info to other websites. Craigslist has been around for ages and is still very useful. Rent-o-meter is great pricing your rental.

3. **Showing the Property:** This is a useful time to prescreen your potential tenants, as well as set expectations for both the tenant and the landlord.

Action Item: It's a great idea to visit sites like Zillow, Craigslist, and Facebook "Buy, sell, trade, groups." You can see how your competition advertises their properties. How do their pictures and pricing stack up to your rentals? Get any new ideas? A little bit of professionalism goes a long way in advertising. You want to get possible tenants in the door and the property will sell itself.

"Competition is a good thing, it forces us to be our best." -Nancy Pearcey

CHAPTER 17

Tenant Screening

There's an old landlords' saying about the three T's being a pain in their backside. "Tenants, toilets, and taxes." The three T's, man. Tenants, toilets, and taxes can definitely be a pain in the ass. We like tenants and toilets though; these are two things we can control in our rental portfolio more than most other factors. The tenants we control via tenant screening, selecting proper tenants, and training/incentivizing the behavior we want. The toilets, short for maintenance, we control via the quality of our rehab. We control the people that do the work and repairs for us. That's why we dive into tenants and toilets, because those are two things you can control in your rental portfolio.

Property Management Software

After we determine rent and get the property advertised, we deal with tenant screening. Right now, we have a property manager that does that for us. However, in the past we've used websites like MySmartMove.com, Cozy.co and Avail.co. Both of these platforms work great. Now even Zillow does it with Zillow Rental Manager. They're amazing tools. They can collect rent for you. You can download applications or use their application process which is sent to you through their rental manager portals. They have slightly different processes and functionality. Take a look at them and pick out what works for you. Again, that's Cozy, Zillow, MySmartMove, and Avail. There are probably other ones too. These generally work through Trans-union or other credit reporting agencies. We love them because they pull credit as well as financial history and criminal background checks.

They typically charge around $35 for an application. However, you can pass this cost on to the tenant, and have them pay the $35 for the application which covers the screening. That's a great way to do it, no cost out of your own pocket. It just takes maybe an hour or two of your time to review the results. It also keeps information private, because you only get what you need for the application. They pay for it, which verifies them. It creates an agreement with you and them, it's pretty neat.

When we were the property managers, Cozy was a tool we enjoyed using. The rent collection feature was super convenient. We'd collect rent payments online rather than them sending us a check. Of the three that we mentioned, Cozy fit our needs best. There are definitely other property management software out there that are very helpful. It really comes down to shopping around and finding a program that suits you best.

If you already own rentals and you're wanting to buy more, then at some point you'll probably need a property management software to scale efficiently. There's a lot of software to choose from. Some software is localized and can only be accessed by your own individual computer. There's cloud-based software. Some of the big ones out there are 'AppFolio' and 'Buildium', we were using one called

PropertyWare. There are probably a hundred of them out there. We think 'AppFolio' probably has the biggest market share. There's a bunch of services out there. Some have free versions with limited functionality, some provide more bells and whistles. Generally speaking, the more functionality you need, the higher the monthly cost. Higher priced programs should be able to do ACH rent/ security deposit collections, and tenant applications/screening.

If you're thinking of managing your own properties on a much larger scale, Appfolio and Buildium both had approximately 100 door minimums. One of them wanted to be triple that before they'd take us on as a client. There are some programs that are designed for much fewer properties. Cozy.co, Avail.co, My Rent, MySmartMove, are some really good transitional programs.

We found Mysmartmove three or four years ago by googling 'How do I do my own tenant screening?' It advertised Trans Union as being the owner or partner of Mysmartmove. So we decided to start there. It was so easy. We literally entered the name and e-mail address of a tenant. Then it had us check a couple of boxes, then the applicants got an email for the application. We got on the phone and told the applicant to check their email. The email said that our company was requesting them to be an applicant. They filled out the application, put in their credit card information. Then boom, 20 minutes later we had all the info we needed. It was so easy to use.

When we set up the tenant screening process, we always try to make more than one person come at the same time. We like to spend our time wisely, rather than running over to the property every time somebody wants to see it. We schedule a time and do showings in batches. We'll tell all interested parties that we're showing the property on Saturday at 10am, or something like that. It saves our time and energy. We don't want to drive over there ten times. Also, it creates a sense of urgency for the applicants when there are several people looking at the property at the same time. If you get ten people in there, think of it this way; two or three of those people might be very interested. They're going to go home and fill out the application right away, rather than waiting a day or two. They're going to be thinking about how there were several other people looking at the place and want it too. They want to get their application in first.

With Cozy, we would print off a little file with a picture of the property, a couple of details, then the URL link to their application. The Cozy URL had the property's extension or number behind it. They could go out and fill Cozy's application. We tell the applicants that they're not paying us. They're paying that application fee to a third party to run their credit and background check. That, in and of itself, is a filtering process. We only want serious people to apply. We don't want the money from the application fee. That's not the point. We're not here to take their money. We suggest that if they think that something in their past is going to come up on the check, we want them to let us know. We'll let them know whether or not they should even apply or not. We have to abide by fair housing standards and regulations. We strongly advise that you do the same. Just do that and you shouldn't have any problems.

We do proper renovations, rather than half-assing our projects. We use techniques we refer to as "tenant proofing". By that, we mean we use certain types of materials that will last longer and be more durable. We do a lot of preventative maintenance too. It only makes sense that we would screen for good tenants too. Selecting and screening tenants is so important to the long-term viability of our rental model. A well-maintained house with good tenants is a great combination. Some of these services we mentioned actually give you a thumbs up or a thumbs down on a possible tenant, which is great. It makes it really easy if you're not good at analyzing numbers. So rather than just giving you a scale that you might not understand, they just tell you if it's a good tenant or not.

Tenant Screening

When we meet a prospective tenant for the first time, we start informally screening them right away. We glance in their cars. Somebody's car is kind of a sneak peek into their life. A way to think of it is, most people's living rooms probably look like their cars. If there is shit and trash everywhere, then that's probably how your house is going to look after they move in. We always take a peek in their car.

Story time with Mike: I love it. It's a great idea. I wish I had thought of that when I was dating my current wife. She loves stuff everywhere. I like things more simplistic and emptier. I like nothing on the shelves, nothing on the walls, boring works for me. We've rejected people from the trashiness and lack of respect they had for their own possessions. If they don't take care of their own possessions, why would they take care of ours? People take better care of their stuff than they will someone else's. That's just human nature in general.

Next, we ask them if they own a vacuum cleaner. It's a simple question that you wouldn't think to ask. However, if they don't own a vacuum cleaner, imagine how nasty the floors are going to be after 30 days, let alone one or two years! This is a big picture thing. If they don't own a vacuum that means one of two things; either, they're hiring somebody to clean their house which is doubtful, or they're not cleaning their house. Asking if they own a vacuum can give you some insight into their world. Something we don't do but might in the future is signing leases in their current residences. We have other landlord friends that do this because they want to come into their home and see how that tenant is treating it or respecting it. If they go to sign a lease and the carpet is torn up, or there are holes in the drywall, then they might not be a good fit. This is more of an advanced strategy, and not something you have to do, or that we even do at the moment. It's just another way to build rapport and do additional screening on your tenants. If the tenants didn't have a clean or a decent looking house, we would probably say we're not interested in renting them the house.

Look in their cars, ask if they own vacuum cleaners, possibly meet them at their house to sign a lease with them. They might have pets they haven't told you about. We're cool with dogs, but we charge a deposit and "pet rent" (usually an extra $25/month). We also ask questions like, "Do you live around here? You work around here? What do you do for work? Who will be living in the house with you? Will any other adults be on the application with you?" These are just some ideas to prescreen your tenants in ways that an application can't really tell you.

There are some other things we look for on an application that might be red flags or indicate that they're not the ideal tenant. If they have a lot of previous addresses, and/or they didn't stay at those addresses for a full year or several years, it seems suspect. If they're bouncing around, we don't really want them as a tenant. We don't want someone we think is going to move out in twelve months. We'd rather get a tenant that can stay in the home for two or three years. We've had tenants stay for five or more years in certain properties. It's great not having to deal with turn over. Typically, there's less maintenance too, because they're not moving in and out and tearing things up.

Something else to look for is evictions. We don't want to deal with people that have had a habit of getting evicted. We want to see their credit score. Is it good, mediocre, or bad? A credit score can tell us if they're good at paying on time and paying off their debts. Last but not least, we check their criminal history. We personally don't care much if they have DWI's, or weed charges, or stuff that doesn't matter much to us. However, if they have a prior rape charge, theft, or a history of violence, we don't rent to people like that. The neighbors are not going to be happy with that. Ask them before they even apply. If they say something along those lines might pop up, then just tell them they might not be a good fit.

Another thing we would highly recommend is asking for references, especially from previous landlords. It's probably not hard for a tenant to give you a bullshit reference. We always call references too. We ask their references questions that people wouldn't typically ask, just to make sure everything made sense. For example, if it was a high school friend or a college friend, we could ask, "How long have you known that person? Have you/ would you ever let this person sleep over at your house? Or stay the week or the weekend? How did that experience go?" We try to make it funny and start laughing with them. We build rapport with the reference, so they'll get their guard down a bit. They'll start telling you what you need to hear, "Yeah, so and so is super clean and a neat freak." Or, "Actually, I don't really like that guy. He passed out on my couch and stole my sweater."

If we get answers we don't want to hear, we're probably not going to put that application on the top of our stack. We're not saying that any of this is necessarily make or break or doesn't work for us. However, if we have better opportunities, we can look elsewhere.

Screen the applicants and screen the applications. There's lots of ways to get information about what a tenant is going to be like before you let them live at your rental property. Some people freeze up when you say you're going to run a credit check and criminal background. We're not looking for perfect angels, we just don't want violent crimes. We're not looking for perfect credit, we're just looking for somebody that can pay the rent.

Some things pop up where you have to make a judgement call. Maybe they had a bankruptcy 12 years ago. People can change their lives. New chapters open and old chapters close. We're not looking for things that would make it impossible to rent to people. We're looking for red flags. Things happen to people and that's okay. We're just trying to home in on a pattern of behavior. Remember, our goal is to provide sound quality housing at a good price for a profit. We're not doing this for free. And if we pick a tenant that can't afford the rent, or won't pay the rent, or tears up our house, then we can't make a profit. It then becomes an unsustainable business model. We care about our tenants. If we care about our tenants, they'll care about our property, and they'll want to remain tenants for a long time. We want our tenants to be happy. These are just things to consider. It's the same way we go about picking contractors, and property management companies. We want to find people we can work with for a long time and develop a win-win relationship going forward.

Let's say you get all the way to the point where you give somebody an application, they fill it out, they pay the fee to run all the credit and background checks, and they decide it's a great deal. You've gotten some insight into their personal lives by how they treat their car, house, or what their references have told you. You've collected the security deposit, first month's rent, and the lease is signed. Then, you give them access to the property, and the keys. Next is managing those tenants. You have to set some expectations. We have what's called a tenant guideline. It's basically the rules of conduct. We might have quiet hours after a certain time because I don't want the cops called. We'll provide them with a sheet with the utilities, names, and numbers. We lay out best practices and expectations. If they want to have a BBQ at 4pm that's all good. However, we're not okay with them having a loud party at 4am. We're not telling them they can't live their life, but we do need them to follow certain guidelines.

We like to go over these guidelines during the lease signing. We go over expectations. We also provide them with contact info; like how to get a hold of us, or who they should contact if there's a problem with the property at 2am, if it's an emergency. If it's not urgent, we can have them wait till the next day. We go over what constitutes an emergency. If the pipes are broken and they're blasting out water everywhere, that's definitely an emergency and we want them to call immediately. Right then and there, even if it's 3 am. Call us and call a plumber if you have to.

Leases

When you get through the application process, and either you or your property manager select somebody that would be a good fit, we like to get them to sign a lease. We typically won't have them sign a lease unless they have the first month's rent, and their security deposit. We need both. This is very important. Sometimes people want to put down just a security deposit, but they don't want to move in for three weeks. To us, that's lost rent. So we basically say all or none. When they sign the lease, it starts right then and there. We will happily prorate days, so they're only paying the rent for the part of the month they start living in the property. But we won't sign a lease and say it starts next Tuesday. If they sign the lease today, they can move in today, otherwise it is available until the next best person comes along with funds. We don't play that waiting game with people. It's the first month's rent, usually prorated, and a deposit at the time they sign. That's it.

We have a lease that we use, and it's very simple. It lays out some simple things; how long is the term? What's the rate going to be? Where and how they pay? Then of course there are other things that lay out their responsibility, our responsibility, and how to handle arbitration. That's our agreement, and it's done in writing. These are standard items among all leases.

Here are some pro tips to put in your lease. Make it very clear that while the property is being controlled by the tenant, the windows are their responsibility. If somebody comes by and throws a brick through that window, even if it's not the tenant that broke it, it's still their responsibility. Sometimes, tenants break windows, or other things in the house out of spite. It can happen. That stuff needs to be included in the lease, especially windows. Another tip involves maintenance calls. Maintenance calls typically have a minimum $50 charge to us just to show up and make an assessment. We make it so they're responsible for $30 of that charge. This prevents them calling when it's something stupid and minor. They think they need a handyman to change a light bulb. That's fine, but we're going to charge them $30. We will pay for anything that's broken or needs repair while we're there and fix those items. However, we're going to charge them that small fee when we have to come out or hire someone to come out. We make that very clear. Those things will be in the lease. Every person can have a different lease. We'll provide a sample lease in this book. We'll also put it in the companion course to this book. www.FreelandLordCourse.com

Right now, with our property manager, we have migrated to the board standard rental contract or lease agreement. Our property manager is taking care of it for us at this point. We recommend that if your goal is to scale your business, then it's critical to outsource the property management part of it. The BRRRR method is all about rapid growth. It can be difficult to scale if you have too many responsibilities within your company.

Follow Up

We like to establish a relationship with our tenants. We've met them at the property, and now we have more of a working relationship. After they've moved into the property for a couple of days or a week, we like to be proactive and ask, "How's it going? Is there anything with the property that needs to be addressed?" Whenever they sign the lease, we ask that they make a list of any issues they have with the property after moving into the property.

It's also really important to take pictures before they move in. More than just showing pictures, we actually take around 150 pictures of a property. We do that when we're buying, and before we rent. We take a lot of pictures, all the angles, every little thing and just throw it in Google Drive or DropBox. This software is free or cheap for how much storage they allow. Take a lot more than you think is necessary, the more the better. The reason is, when the tenant moves out, and you put together a list of all those repairs, you can look at your photos and question them about whether something was broken or not before they moved in. They'll probably always say it was like that when they moved in. However, if you have photo proof it wasn't, that helps your position. Especially if you ever have to go to court for any reason. Now you have evidence and proof. Also, it helps when justifying sending somebody a bill for $800, $1500, or $2000 for the repairs. If you have the before and after photos, it really helps your case.

When a tenant moves in, there's almost always going to be a couple issues with the property. Even a newly rehabbed property is probably going to have three or four things the contractors missed. Maybe a pipe is loose or leaks a little bit. The washing machine might not have been hooked up right, or the AC tube is leaking. Whatever it is, we just tell them to make a list and we'll get somebody out there to take care of any issues with the property. That way we're getting ahead of the maintenance. We're telling them that we want them to be happy with the property. We're a landlord that wants to maintain the property. We're setting the expectation on what's going to happen.

We've never done this personally, but our property managers do this for us, and set up an annual inspection, whether they moved out or not. Some people even do it more frequently. We think that getting inside a property once a year is plenty. We just want to evaluate the property. We say we're checking for maintenance issues that need to be addressed. We don't want to have a tenant for 5-10-15 years, then find out they're a hoarder, or destroying our property. We're not there, so we don't know what's going on unless we get in somehow. We have our property manager do it once a year. It gives you a chance to meet your tenants, see inside the property, and build rapport again. As a landlord we have that right. We put that into the lease that we have the ability to do that. Sometimes you have to give them 24 hours written notice.

It's important to manage your tenants and maintain your properties. We also like to do a drive by of the exteriors every few months or have someone on our team do it. We want to make sure the outside is taken care of, that the lawn is mowed, etc. We can have them take pics if necessary.

Managing Tenants

Until you have ten doors, you probably don't need a property manager. In fact, you should really try doing it on your own just for the experience. Ten doors is a great

"You have to be compassionate but take no

breaking point. A reason for that, is you'll learn what the property manager has to deal with when dealing with tenants. It's a lesson you can't learn without doing it. You're going to get calls in the middle of the night, and deal with certain inconveniences.

You'll learn to be compassionate and objective with people. A lot of tenants are "professional tenants". They know how to game the system, and how to game their landlords. Those people have tactics they'll use against you. They might use your emotions against you. They'll constantly have a sob story for you. You'll hear a lot of sad stories. A lot of it is true, a lot of it is just life, and a lot of it is just BS. You have to be compassionate but take no shit. You can be understanding, but keep in mind that you're not running a charity. This is a business. You have to run it like a business to provide for your family. You can't afford to pay someone else's rent. If they don't want to, or can't pay you, you're paying someone else's rent for them if you don't collect rent. That's not the business we're in, we don't play that game.

Something we learned from a property manager is to file for eviction if they're ten days late with rent. They get a couple days grace period, where we don't charge late fees. Start the eviction process after ten days. If they get the rent caught up prior to the day of the scheduled hearing, you can drop the case, no harm, no foul. They owe you the cost to file that. That's in our lease as well. That's something we're very big on. It makes people realize you are serious about collecting your rent. We file it on day ten or eleven. Even if they call us saying they are enroute with the money. People that are habitually late with rent, or not paying at all, are probably lying. They could have a sob story about being on their way, then they got a blown-out tire. That's typically what happens, that's how it works. It's frustrating not being able to trust people. But you'll notice patterns with untrustworthy people.

On the tenth of the eleventh we file the eviction notice. It costs them $289, so we just call it $300 and we bill it back to them, even if they pay the rent. We'll happily close the file. But it's their cost to file, and it's in the lease. It's stated right there. We're not the type of people that it is okay to pay late rent to.

Ten days is a good enough grace period. We don't even start charging late fees until day five. We also make it very clear when we are signing the lease, we tell them about our late pay policy and how important it is to get it paid before day 10 or it is going to cost them an extra $300.

We're doing the BRRRR method. We're buying, rehabbing, renting, and re-financing. We have notes on these properties that we have to pay back. These properties are not free. We can't give free rent to people. We're paying rent to the bank, aka a mortgage. The bank needs their money too. By lending us money, they have an opportunity cost to where they could have invested that money somewhere else. So even though they're paying money to us as a landlord, we still have a lot of expenses we need to cover like the mortgage, insurance, property taxes, maintenance, management fees. Make sure your tenants get their rent paid. Everyone's a little different about their late fees, and tolerances. However, we've noticed that if you're not serious about collecting rent, the tenants take advantage of that.

Problem Tenants

Problem tenants, who are they, and how do you deal with them? This is really situational. It depends on what's going on. At this point, we have a property manager that takes care of these issues for us. That's what we recommend for you once you own enough properties. You don't want to have to deal with these issues. We like to deal with the property, but we don't like dealing with the people. If you're at the stage where you're still managing your own, no big deal. We've been there, we're still dealing with a couple of tenants. Some tenants are going to be easier to deal with than others. Some are going to be a huge pain in the ass. Some you're even going to have to evict. We don't want this to be a surprise for you, because you're probably going to come across it eventually. When a tenant quits paying, you have to kick them out. It's going to happen. The more properties you have, and the longer you've been doing it, the higher chance that you're going to have to do this more frequently. These are people, but this is also a business. It's important that you run your business properly. Make sure they know this is a business to you. You need to be objective, and stern with people, especially in certain areas. But at the same time, they're human beings so you want to treat them with dignity and respect too. We like to handle tenant issues one at a time. When something arises, we ask them, "What's the problem? How can we help you? Let's solve it together." That's the mindset we usually have. We like to ask the tenant if they have a solution in mind. Oftentimes, the tenant's solution is a cheaper and quicker solution than we might suggest. For example, the windows are the tenant's responsibility. One might have broken that they can't afford to fix right now. It might cost less to put a piece of plywood over a broken window and wait three months for them to get it fixed, rather than whatever solution we would have come up with. They know their situation better than we do but might be afraid to speak their mind.

We thank them for letting us know what's going on. We want to address this together and see if they have any suggestions. We want to make sure that we keep the integrity of the house and their safety in mind. So, if they have a broken door, or a broken window, that's probably a bit more of a priority than a sink that's dripping. When it comes to repairs, we definitely prioritize some things over others. We want to convey to our tenants that there will be a fee, or a cost associated with maintenance, though. We're happy to come over and fix things. However, we want to set the precedent from the beginning, that it's not okay for them to call us every day with every little thing. We've heard it all. "The door's rubbing, the toilet is running, the doorknob is loose, etc. That's fine. These are simple problems that we can address one by one, however it takes time and energy to get out to a property. There's a cost associated with us coming out. That's the way we like to do it. Some property managers don't necessarily charge the tenant, but they're going to charge the owner of the property to deal with those things. We like to set it up from the beginning to let the tenants know that there will be a charge. It's not a big charge, around $30. Think of it this way; if it's something they can easily fix themselves for $30 bucks or less, they would probably rather do themselves than have somebody walk through their home. It's just a form of incentive to eliminate the little knick knack stuff from them calling and bothering you with. We're just implying that if we need to come out and fix something on the property, we want there to be a real reason. If it's something legit, we might not even charge them a service call. However, if we have to come out for some petty little BS item, then we're definitely charging. We're not trying to avoid or defer maintenance. We just want to instill in the tenants a better idea of discretion.

There's a clear difference between a hole in the roof or the AC going out, or whatever, versus the blinds not going up all the way or a tree that's blowing in the wind and rubbing up against the window. That's on them to take care of simple stuff. If a screen is broken, that's not a big deal. But if there's water leaking, or the house is on fire, that is a big deal. We need them to call us. We need to know about those things ASAP. A slumlord might push tenants away by not working with them to address property issues. However, a pushover is never going to make money in this business either. There's a happy medium. We plan on working together with our tenants, so we can keep them there for a long time. We'd rather spend a little extra money to keep somebody happy. If we can keep them in the property for three to five years or more, that money spent is actually less in the grand scheme of things than going the cheap route. Long term tenants are a gold mine because there's less opportunity cost, vacancies, and repairs we have to make, compared to having to get a new tenant. It's a pain fixing up a property after a tenant leaves, and then paying a property manager to lease it.

Once you get up to a certain number of tenants, you're going to run into problem tenants. Even if you screened properly, and did your due diligence, it's merely a matter of time before you get a tenant that's not worth having. They might be someone who calls once a month for a maintenance issue and makes a big deal out of it each time. If they're not taking care of your property, or they're consistently coming up with excuses as to why rent is late. At the end of their lease, don't let them come back. Fire your tenant. It's as simple as that. Tell them you're not renewing their lease. A lot of leases have a 30-day notice clause if the tenant wants to move out. However, we can also give them a 30 days' notice to vacate the property. This is clearly more of a last resort option. We just want you to know that it is an option. It's something to consider if you're in certain areas where that may be required.

Rent Collection

Another aspect of managing tenants is rent collection. The old-fashioned way of collecting rent is having the landlord come knocking and asking for the rent checks. People also write checks for rent, and mail them in. That's definitely a bit old school. Not everyone is doing that anymore. The easier way is to use an online service like Cozy.co, Zillow rental manager, or My Smart Move.

With these services, you can set up the tenants in a little portal so they can pay their rent online every month. It pulls directly from their bank account and deposits the money directly in yours. It saves everybody a bit of a headache. There's a log of it that everyone can see, and there's no checks lost in the mail. That's our preferred way. We're actually working on making it a requirement for all our tenants to do ACH direct deposits. We're working with our property manager to push all of our tenants to do that. Collecting rent can be an issue if you don't have a system in place. We want to make sure everyone pays their rent, and it's easy for us to see who has and who hasn't.

If for whatever reason, a tenant is behind on rent after the third day, we call them, and say, "We noticed that we didn't get your rent yet. What's going on?" We want to know if that rent isn't coming in, or if it is, when we can expect it. With that said, on the tenth day we let them know that we start filing the eviction process. There are almost no exceptions for that with us. We literally file on anyone who does not pay the rent by the tenth. We have to collect the money. This is really important.

That's why we go with a one-year lease mostly. Our property manager only does one-year leases for that reason. However, we do offer price breaks sometimes for tenants that sign two-year leases. We love doing that. Let's say a property rents for $875/month. We will usually throw it out there when we're doing a showing with them. We might say, "If you want to do a two-year lease instead of one, it'll only be $825/month. We'll knock $50 a month off the rent. The math comes out to $50 times 12 months equaling $600. We get $600 less a year on that property. However, with just a one-month vacancy we'd lose $875 in that example. Not to mention, we'd have to fix the place back up. So, we usually do a $50 or a $100 discount on more expensive properties because it actually saves us money and headache. We'll be honest, quite often, people end up liking the place and don't want to move after a year anyway. A lot of times they're pleasantly surprised when we offer them a discount for signing a two-year lease. They feel like they won. How about a four-year lease? We'll give them $100 off.

It's just another strategy. There are different ways to do it. No one of them is right or wrong, it's just whatever makes sense for you and your business.

Recap:

1. **Property Management Software:** Zillow, Mysmartmove, and Cozy.co are some very useful pieces of software. They can make tenant screening and rent collection much easier.

2. **Tenant Screening:** We want tenants that will pay rent on time and treat our property with care and respect.

We do this by asking calibrated questions, calling references, looking at how they treat their personal items, and we use a 3rd party for background and credit checks.

3. **Leases:** We're proactive and discuss our expectations from our tenants as well as what they can expect from us. We also discuss utilities and how maintenance calls work.

4. **Follow Up:** We want to make sure the tenants are happy. We ask them to prepare a list of items they need fixed within the first couple of months living at the property.

5. **Managing Tenants:** There's a happy medium when managing tenants. You don't want to be a slumlord, and you don't want to be a pushover either. Focus on a win-win relationship where they're happy, and also taking care of your property.

6. **Problem Tenants:** As you grow your rental portfolio, it's just a matter of time before you deal with problem

tenants. It's best to screen for them in advance or help them work through their problems together. However, eventually you'll have to "fire" a client by not renewing the lease or even evict them.

7. **Rent Collection:** We prefer online payments or ACH. There's plenty of property management software to help with this.

Action Item: Find a 3rd party tenant screening company that works for you. You should be able have a screening done for around $35. Make sure this is paid for by the possible tenants, not you. It's also a good idea to come up with a list of qualifying questions you'd like to ask the possible tenants. Use our ideas or come up with your own.

*"Good management consists of showing average people how to do the work of superior people." -*John D. Rockerfeller.

CHAPTER 18

Property Management

We're going to be focused on the second R of BRRRR in this chapter, rent. More specifically, we'll be focused on the property management aspect of it. Last chapter was about screening tenants, managing the tenants, managing their expectations, managing rent collection, and managing the on-boarding/off-loading of those tenants. Now it's time to talk about property managers, and whether or not you should hire one.

You may or may not hire a property manager. That's something you might save money on in the beginning. But as your business scales, you're definitely going to want someone to manage it. We use a property manager. We got to a point where we needed someone else to help us. It's hard to do both. It's hard to be in acquisition mode and switch to management mode. Maybe one day, we'll build our own property management company; who knows? But for right now, it works great for us to have somebody help with the leasing and the day to day management and rent collection. We'd rather focus our efforts on buying more. It's a full-time job just managing, and it's a full-time job being in acquisitions.

We think ten doors is the magic number for deciding to hire a property manager. However, there are some people that want nothing to do with the people side of the business. That's okay. If you try it and don't like it, then by all means, hire a property manager. If you have the right mindset though, and follow our BRRRR system, you're going to grow rapidly. That's our two cents. If you're not, then you might want to reconsider that mindset. We tend to like dealing with the property and having a property manager to deal with the people. The other day, a buddy of ours asked us, "How do we do it? How are we growing this fast?" We said, we're property guys, the property manager is a people guy. That's exactly how it works. Even when the property manager has maintenance requests, he is dealing with those people. He sends it over to our team and we deal with the property.

Property Management

We think that having ten properties is a great breaking point to switch from being your own property manager to hiring someone, if using the BRRRR strategy. It doesn't matter if you're just slowly doing this. But if you're actively, and aggressively using the BRRRR strategy, that means you're buying a lot of properties. The more you put into your portfolio, getting them through this process, then a property manager becomes an ever-increasing key player. That's somebody you really want to make a good partnership with. Trying to do the property management and acquire a lot of new properties at the same time is going to be tough if not impossible. You can't do it all, Build a Team!

We've tried to do the property management in-house, multiple times. We couldn't make it work for us. We're not even embarrassed to say it. Failure is part of the success formula. We need to stress this more. You have to fail in order to be successful. You certainly don't want big failures that knock you out of the game, but little failures along the road are going to happen. We're not ashamed of it. We've tried two or three different property managers. We even tried bringing one in-house. It wasn't working for us. So, we outsourced that responsibility. We wanted someone who could basically be the CEO of that business unit.

The guy we went with worked on Mike's personal rentals. Mike told the team that this guy is pretty good. The guy came out, we interviewed him, and he's been a rock star for us. We're very happy with him. We've thrown him more properties. We've probably increased his portfolio 50%. It's going to double or triple by the time we're done!

Wealth on Autopilot

We needed a property manager. We couldn't handle doing both, managing property, and aggressively acquiring property. It's difficult to deal with people and property at the same time. We needed laser focus. We have laser focus now, to achieve massive growth, which allows us to be more of a passive investor. That's really the goal here. We want to get checks in the mailbox every month. We want to make money when we sleep. We want to build wealth and take advantage of the tax breaks of owning rental property. Wealth creation is very important to us, even more so than income. People might have a different opinion on that than us. However, we want to build wealth, specifically using real estate. The reason is, we're terrible at saving money. So how do we save more money than most people we know? We put our savings on autopilot. We get a house rented out, so somebody else is paying down that debt. We're building up our equity in that property. It's the exact same thing as putting nickels, dimes, and quarters into a piggy bank every day. That's how we view rental property. We see it as a piggy bank, where we deposit nickels, dimes, and quarters. In 10-15 years, we're going to own a bunch of piggy banks. But rather than being the small clay ones you get at a knick-knack store, these are the size of cars, and they're filled with hundred-dollar bills. The best part is, somebody else is depositing that money for me. If we had to do it, it would never get done. In fact, we would never own any piggy banks. Saving money is also boring, not to mention, it's a challenge to keep up with inflation. Building wealth through rental properties is a great way to ensure wealth down the road.

Buying rental properties, with the strategy we use, we put savings on autopilot. It forces savings upon us. We can't stop the process, even if we wanted to. We can't spend the equity.

"It forces savings upon us. We can't stop the process, even if we wanted to. We can't spend the equity."

Much like you can't get the money in a piggy bank without breaking it. It's beautiful. It's going to create wealth. And if you know your numbers, it's almost guaranteed that you'll build wealth instead of gambling. We're passionate about it.

Property Managers

Property managers, we love them because they allow us to acquire more properties quickly. They allow us to be laser focused on the acquisition side of the business. And that's where we're at. Last year, we've been ramping up our rental game. Now we're about two thirds of the way to our goal. Our goal wasn't eight properties. Our goal is 150! We compare ourselves, and our business strategy to a train. Last year our train was just starting to move. It takes a while for a train to get moving. Same went for us. We made poor choices with our property management. We didn't have that aspect fine-tuned yet. We didn't have all of our banking relationships lined up. We didn't have all of our contractors lined up. We didn't have all that stuff. Now that we've got that all in place, now our train is running. Now we're trying to add a new property once a week. That's our goal. That's huge for us. That might seem like a crazy high goal to most of our students, however, that could be peanuts to somebody else. Everybody has a different goal and ambition. Grant Cardone has 7000 units. If he had to start from scratch, his goal for year one wouldn't be 150, it would be more like 1000. Everybody is going to grow at their own pace.

Everybody starts in a different place and has different ambitions. There's no right or wrong way to do it. We love our goal. We're super excited about it. It's lofty, and challenging, but we know it's doable.

Story Time with Mike: I look at my father. He's a rental investor as well. I don't know how many properties him and his wife have, but it's probably around 30 now. I used to think that was a lot of properties. He was working a full-time job on top of managing them. I watched my dad acquire rentals slowly. It's a great way to do it. He was working a full-time job. He was able to add one or two a year. Now he has probably 25-30 piggy banks. He managed them himself for a long time before switching to a property manager. That was around the time he really wanted to retire to pursue hobbies.

The choice of when to hire a property manager is up to you, as we mentioned before, we think having around 10 rental properties is a good number to switch from self-management of the properties to hired help. It's not set in stone, but rather, a good rule of thumb. It's up to you to figure out what works for you. It takes skill, understanding, and patience to deal with tenants. If you don't like dealing with people, or have a short fuse, it might not even take 10 properties before you realize that managing the properties yourself is not for you.

If you don't have people skills, maybe getting a property manager is the best play for you on day one. The catch 22 is that you don't really know what a property manager does, or what they're dealing with. So, when you have to deal with the property manager, it's going to be more difficult to relate.

There's a lot of value to be your own property manager before hiring one, because you'll have more experience and understanding of what they're doing.

When getting your first property, you have to think to yourself, "What are all the steps in just leasing the property?" It's interesting. That first couple of properties can be overwhelming. However, we have close to 100 properties now and we've got systems in place, and it no longer becomes overwhelming. We can identify where we're at in the process. Are we at the project planning stage, mid renovation, occupancy inspection, marketing to tenants, or ready to refinance? We know where we are at every point, and what needs to happen next. It becomes a simple process. However, it can be difficult to do just one or two. By scaling we actually became more efficient. We really got our freight train moving, so to speak.

When to Hire

It's a personal decision on when to hire. We just want to iterate the pros of doing the work yourself in the beginning as well as the pros of outsourcing later on. It makes sense from a financial standpoint too. It's hard, if not impossible to scale your business. Too early, and you don't have anything to leverage when talking to a property manager. A property manager isn't going to give you a discount for only two properties. They're not going to care. Also, property managers can take a decent chunk of your cash flow. If you're using the rental properties to live off, and that cash flow is paying your bills, then a property manager might not be the best solution. You're paying them for convenience, and that convenience doesn't come free. When we go on wholesale appointments, we tell the sellers that we're "cash buyers". We're offering a convenience to them. What we need in return for that convenience is a discount. We don't need to buy their house. We're clear, transparent, and blunt about that. We're not rude about it, we do it to set the expectation. It's how we screen serious sellers, so we aren't wasting our time or theirs. We're happy to buy it, however we don't really "need" it. We trade a cash offer, which is convenience, for a discount.

It's the same thing with a property manager. They're providing convenience. We don't have to worry about the leasing anymore, or maintenance calls. However, we're trading them a piece of the pie. That give and take will always be there. Convenience is a big thing. A property manager provides convenience by taking over a lot of responsibilities of managing tenants for you.

We do want to point out, just because you hire a property manager, doesn't mean you are done managing. Instead of managing tenants, you have to manage the manager, person, entity or whatever. We also recommend you check in with your property manager from time to time and discuss updates as well as set up a maintenance plan for your properties if they didn't lay one out for you when you signed up with them. This is a longer-term plan, but you don't want your properties to fall apart over the 10, 20, or 30+ years you own them.

Most property managers charge around 10%. When you have more properties, it is easier to negotiate a bit lower rate or discount as you're bringing more cash in for them. Remember though, cheaper isn't always better. One thing to be aware of is how property managers earn more money. Yes, the 10% is just the beginning.

There are two other ways they make money; Leasing and Maintenance. Ask what they charge to lease a property. It could be anywhere from $1000 flat rate to ½ a month's rent or even a full month's rent. We pay about ½ months' rent.

The next way is the way they make money is something you really need to pay attention to. They also make money through maintenance requests. They may have in-house maintenance workers that are going to charge you, the owner, $100. However, they may only pay the worker $20 for a service call. They profit from service calls. This can be a big conflict of interest. You want to align your goals with the property manager.

In the first two ways that property managers make money (percentage of rent collected and a fee for leasing out a property) the higher the rent, the better it is for you and your property manager. However, in the third way property managers make money (charging you for maintenance calls), now you can be in a conflict of interest. The more calls made, the more money they make, and the more you pay them. Pay attention to this! This could be one of the biggest factors to your long-term success. Our property manager does not make any money on service calls! This is HUGE for us, and we recommend you look closely at how any property manager bills for maintenance very carefully before signing up with them to manage for you. We suggest looking for a mid-size property manager. An individual or smaller company that manages around 150 units. There you have someone with systems in place but still will know you personally if you bring them 5-10 units to manage. Much smaller managers might not be able to scale up. Much larger managers might make you feel like a small fish and you might not get attention when requested.

What to Expect

More pros and cons. The property managers are a business. They're profiting off us. We're just paying them for convenience. We don't want to take the calls. We don't want to do the maintenance, or the leasing. We just don't like dealing with tenants in general. We'd rather buy the property and let them deal with those issues. They're professional. They already have their processes and systems in place. That can be difficult to achieve just starting out. It's a bit of a learning curve of what you need to get together. However, now we've got things in place, like a checklist for a walk through, a lease agreement that we use over and over again, hundreds of times. A good property manager will have a process too. They'll have an application process. They'll already have their software chosen, and familiarized. They know what they like, and they're using it.

All these systems work relatively the same. There's not really one better than the other one. Some interfaces just work better for different personality types. However, there are so many to choose from, it can be overwhelming. However, our property manager doesn't need to go through that struggle or learning curve anymore. We can hand him a property at basically any level. We could give him one that needs $40k worth of rehab, and he could handle it. Or, we could give him one that has an occupancy inspection, and the maids are leaving as he is walking in. These decisions are made by the cost to provide that convenience. We prefer to hand it off as the maids are walking out, or the inspector is in the parking lot writing up a report. We like to line them up, so the transition goes smoothly, and we don't kill time in between.

They are also pros for tax time. Property managers, especially the ones that use some legit software will be able to send out 1099's. We'll know exactly how much rent we collected, and how much our expenses were. Then we go to our accountant and give them a piece of paper. It's so much easier than going through a shoe box full of receipts or spreadsheets. Property managers will really simplify your taxes. That's huge!

Property management software typically has an accounting program built right into that software. The software just spits out the data you need, it's awesome.

Another thing that you should expect, and almost demand from your property manager is, a written statement with your owner draw each month. We're very passionate about this. A lot of property management software sucks when it comes to reporting. They can be terrible, even some of the best ones out there. Often, they give you a 36-page report for a property that is almost impossible to read. Instead, we make our property manager create a simple excel spreadsheet that shows the dates, amounts, and the reasons for money going in or out. That's it. It's how we do our taxes too. That way, we can see at the end of the month if someone didn't pay rent. Or if there was a maintenance call, what it was, where it was, and what was collected. We don't want to dig through 60 different reports, like accounts receivables. There's too many, one for late rents, one for maintenance, etc. It's just too hard to understand. We make it a requirement when we hire them, to send us an easy to understand report at either the beginning or end of the month, whenever they distribute their owner draws. This is very important. If the numbers aren't simplified, it can be very confusing. It's not their intention to be misleading. However, we've seen them all before. Almost every property management software makes reports that are very difficult to read. So we make it the job of the property manager to help out with simplifying the reports. We need to keep an eye on what's coming in, and what's going out.

Maintenance

We typically handle maintenance with a phone call. Sometimes we get an email, it depends on if we're using a property management software. Either way, calls, etc. are going to come into you or your property manager. In our case, we have people that we're already working with; contractors, general contractors, sub-contractors, etc. that we'll send out to help us do those maintenance items. Then we will pay those people directly. We may or may not bill back the tenant. If you're dealing with a property management company, they'll probably have their own maintenance people.

Just because you hire a property manager, doesn't mean you're not managing anymore. Maintenance is the main thing that needs to be looked at and managed when dealing with a property manager. Maintenance is actually a profit center for a lot of property managers. A typical rate for a property manager is 8-12% of the rent. It could be different in other parts of the country. Most people don't know this, but only about 50% of a property manager's business income comes from the actual management fee. The rest of it comes from the mark up of their services. So, with maintenance, they're going to mark up the materials and labor. If they send somebody out to do a $100 repair; they might bill you $300. Knowing that it's such a huge profit center for them, you might want to do the maintenance yourself, or at least make sure you're working with somebody you really trust. Our goal isn't to make you paranoid or distrusting, but rather, to make you cautious and aware. If you've hired a property manager to handle the maintenance issues that's okay, just make sure you stay on top of them and you manage those expenses. A couple of bad maintenance things can throw off your cash flow for the entire year. Most people don't realize that property managers can have a financial incentive to rack up a maintenance bill. We're lucky that we have one that doesn't, and we handle our own maintenance.

We have a hybrid model with our property manager. We pay 8%, which is on the low side. However, we have him take care of leasing. He gets 75% of the first month's rent for getting a new tenant. That can be another profit center. Leasing is something that takes time. We don't want to deal with that.

We want him to deal with the tenants, we'll take care of the property. He makes 75% of the first month's rent. Any maintenance calls he gets, is included in his 8% fee. He's just the communicator. He sends it over to us and we work with the sub-contractors to address the issue. That's how our business operates. Yours might be different. You just have to figure out what works best for you. We like to deal with the property, and we like him to deal with the people.

There is going to be maintenance on your properties, even if you have just rehabbed it. It happens. It happens ten out of ten times. In St Louis, the summer can be pretty hot, and we get a lot of AC service calls. They're not fun to hear. We hate having to replace another system, because they're so expensive. As we mentioned before, if those systems are super old when you buy a property, you may want to go ahead and replace them before you get a tenant. Fix that glitch in advance. It's not fun for you, and it's not fun for the tenant.

Let's run through just a couple of things that you should basically be expecting, like Leaky faucets and Doors are not completely closing. Your service calls are going to be seasonal as well. We know that sounds weird, but they are. A few months ago, we were dealing with multiple calls of leaking basements. That was spring though. It was raining constantly. So why do we get so many leaky basements? Two reasons, either the gutters are clogged, or there is a drainage issue on the property itself. The slope of the land, or the gutters are not being diverted away from the foundation. Those are pretty frequent problems.

Air conditioner issues are a pretty frequent, and seasonal issue. Here in St Louis, temperatures fluctuate wildly, and all of sudden people all have their AC issues on the same day. We get hammered with air conditioner service requests in a short period of time. It really depends when the tenant decides to kick that AC on, and how cold they like it. But eventually those AC's go out and they need to be replaced or serviced. So, we have had a ton of those.

We want to be compassionate with the tenants because they're living there. We want them to live in a nice home. But we have to have some tough skin in this business. Sometimes tenants give us lip on the phone. They can give us an attitude. If you're dealing with 40-80-100 properties, you can't just drop what you're doing and get out there. There might be a 24-48 hour waiting period before you can put them in a proper place on your priority list. We tell them we'll get there when we can, but we might have other pressing matters.

It's a fine line that you have to be cautious about. You want people to let you know when there's a serious issue. We appreciate them calling, and we tell them that. But we have to establish priorities. We can't and shouldn't address every issue right away. We tell them, we'll get to it when we can get to it. People come off rude. They'll yell about how they're paying $1200-1400/month to live there, and their shower head is dripping. That is one small problem that we're going to work on and get fixed when we can. But other things can be a lot more pressing. A lot of the small things, we just brush off. Again, we want to be sympathetic. Heat going out in the winter, or AC going out in the summer is a big deal. A leaky shower head can wait.

If it's freezing cold in the winter and the furnace goes out, sometimes we can't get the HVAC guy out for three days. In these cases, we've brought out several space heaters for them. We've even paid for people's hotel rooms. We're going to do what it takes to make them happy with us. We actually care about people. But at the same time, we limit the amount of expenses that we have to incur, because we're running a business. We strive to find that happy medium to where we have a good tenant landlord relationship, that's what we're looking for.

Here's an example of working with a tenant. We had a tenant ask if they could get a 220 volt plug for their electric dryer. This was before the tenant moved in. We asked for a list. We wanted it before they moved in, because it would be cheaper, more efficient, quicker, all of the above if the house was still vacant. We could just give the contractor the lockbox code. But after they move in, we'd have to coordinate with them and the contractor, which could be more difficult. Somebody else asked for lattice fencing around their deck to make it look prettier and keep critters out. We did it. It's part of building the landlord tenant relationship. We want the tenant to be happy. For about $100, we made a tenant very happy.

We went out of our way to install an electrical line to plug in for their drier. We went out of our way to do the lattice fence for a deck. It's a way to show we care, because we do. It's not a big deal. We've done a lot of things to strengthen our relationship with our tenants. This is great because if we haven't received their rent some month, we can call and say, "We're not trying to bother you, but haven't received your rent yet." They're almost always eager to scratch your back since you scratched theirs. Then they get it to us right away. That's the type of good relationship between the tenant and landlord that we're trying to create. We want to keep them happy, so we can get our rent on time, and keep the place occupied.

We pay, between 8-12% for a company to manage the property. By that, we mean showing the property, accepting tenant applications, collecting rent, handling financial statements, etc. There's a lot of overhead involved in that part of the business. However, that's where they make only half their profit. The other half comes from fees based on property maintenance. When we first started using property managers, we tried a couple of them out. We put a cap on their maintenance repairs. We determined what level of spending they were allowed to do without talking to us. You might not want them to do any maintenance without talking to you first, until you're comfortable with them. We typically set the cap around $100-250 to start. We want them to use discretion and make their own judgement calls. We don't want to be bothered about every little repair. That's why we hired a property manager in the first place. However, we do not want them to spend more than $250 of our money without talking to us first.

For example, if it's a leaky faucet or sink, we don't want them to replace the faucet every time. That cost would add up. However, if it's a recurring problem we might rather fix the whole problem, and get it done once, rather than sending a repair guy out there several times at $100 each time. We want to know how they're handling the maintenance, to make sure it's in our best interest. It all comes down to experience and discretion.

Something to keep in mind is that sometimes cutting a corner is more expensive in the long run. In fact, it's more expensive most of the time. So rather than having an HVAC guy come out every three months to do maintenance, we'll probably bite the bullet and buy a new one. We know that we'll spend three times more money over a five-year period by sending that guy out every 90 days to service it, rather than just replacing it. That's something to keep in mind. The property manager might not care about you having a top of the line furnace. Some might be greedy and enjoy the extra money they get from the service calls. Or they just might not know any better. Either way, it's your property, your money, and thus your responsibility.

Unfortunately, when dealing with rental properties, it's kind of a nickel and dime business. We need to make sure we're keeping an eye on those little expenses, because a lot of little expenses can turn into big expenses. It's easy to think that since some of these properties' average cash flow is around $300, we should be well in the clear of making a steady profit. However, if our property management fees are through the roof, our cash flow could be neutral or even net negative by the end of the year. It's crucial to manage the property managers.

Definitely try managing your properties on your own at first. We recommend you do that just so you can get a feel for it. You can learn it, and understand what it's like dealing with the tenants, the leasing, maintenance, and possibly what it's like dealing with an eviction on your own. These are good things to learn. A property manager is used to help you grow and scale your business when you get to that point. However, they provide that convenience at a cost.

Recap:

1. **Property Management:** We think everyone should manage their first 10 or so properties. It's a great experience. This involves screening tenants, signing leases, collecting rent, and handling maintenance calls.

2. **Wealth on Autopilot:** We got into this business to build wealth. At some point in time, to really scale your

business, you're going to want to hire a property manager.

3. **Property Managers:** Property managers provide a convenient service for a profit. Make sure their interests are in line with yours.

4. **When to Hire:** We think around ten units is ideal. Less than that, and the property management fees eat too much into your profit. More than that, you'll focus too much energy on property management, and not enough on property acquisition.

5. **What to Expect:** A property manager should really help your business run smoother. However, you still have to manage the managers. Good communication when hiring and during the on-boarding process is crucial.

6. **Maintenance:** No matter how well you prepare the property for tenants, things get in disrepair, especially seasonal items like the HVAC. Be proactive. Work with your tenants to make them happy, but don't be a

pushover. Also, watch out for this being a profit center for property management companies.

Action Item: Network with other investors. Ask around on social media or REIA's who other investors use for property managers, and what their experiences have been. Even if you're not ready to hire yet, it's best to start with the end in mind. Just by talking to other investors about the topics in this book, you will get a better sense of how to manage your properties and tenants.

"People might not remember exactly what you said or did, but they always remember how you made them feel. That's what matters most." -Tony Hsieh

PART V

REFINANCING

CHAPTER 19

Refinancing

We want to grow our rental portfolio to 150. We don't really have a reason why we picked that number. Maybe because it's lofty, but doable. It's divisible by the three owners. So that's the number we picked, and the number we're going after. We're about a third of the way there. We are close to 50 properties already. Our goal is to get to 150 in the next one to two years. The sooner the better.

This chapter is about refinancing. This is the third R in the BRRRR strategy. We've already covered this a bit, but we're going to dive deeper in this chapter. We're playing a game of chess, not checkers. We have to think well ahead when it comes to building wealth and creating a rental portfolio. It's not a simple one, two, three thing. We don't want to over complicate it. However, we have to know what we're doing when it comes to refinancing with banks. They want to know our history. They want to see what we've done in the past and have confidence that we can run a successful operation. They want to make sure they are betting on a winning horse. They don't want to gamble with their money. They want to know that we can pay them back.

Here's the big picture when using the BRRRR strategy. The refinance part of this is as important as every other piece of the BRRRR strategy. If you're using private funds or hard money to buy the property and rehab that property. You'll need to refinance that house once you get it rented. You need to pay off those hard money lenders or private money lenders for several reasons. First, your initial term with those individuals or companies probably wasn't for three to five years. Those loans are usually short term; usually between four to eight months. The interest rate you're paying those lenders is almost always going to be two to three, or even four times as high of an annual interest compared to the bank you're working with. Bank money is almost always the cheapest money in terms of cost or interest rates. Refinancing out of high interest rate loans into low interest rate loans is very important in the BRRRR strategy. You have to be able to pay those private lenders back. Then you can re-borrow that money and keep the train rolling. Buy the next house, and keep your crews rehabbing.

Getting Started

If you're currently an employee, as in you have a W-2 job, that's super useful when it comes to building your rental portfolio. It's going to really help you refinance with lenders. You need to have at least two years of tax returns doing what you've been doing. We know you probably want to quit your day job, especially if you hate it. We'd love to see you quit and be self-employed too if that is what you want. We want you to live your dreams. However, before you do that, we strongly encourage you sticking it out for a bit. Having those W-2 returns will really help you. Those W-2 returns are worth more than just a paycheck.

If you don't have experience in rental real estate, don't quit that day job yet. We just want to emphasize that point. The banks see you as a lendable person. So, as we said, the BRRRR strategy is a game of chess not checkers. You want to keep that W-2 and apply for loans with as many banks as possible. Apply with as many banks as you can and start that process today. Don't wait until you've bought, rehabbed, and leased a house before talking to a banker about refinancing. You need to be doing all these things at the same time, or even before. Start establishing your relationship with a banker or bankers right now. We personally like to work with a local bank that has between three to five branches. The reason we like these banks is because they're going to lend to us in a style called portfolio lending. That means they're not going to be selling off these mortgages to the secondary market. This is especially important for commercial loans, because those have to be re-underwritten every 3-5 years. We'll discuss why that's important in the section about commercial loans.

Refinancing is super important. Introduce yourself to your local bankers. Make sure they know who you are. If you're not approved today, don't walk out of that bank ashamed and disappointed. We've been denied loans. We still get denied a loan about once a month. But that's because we get loans on lots of things. It happens, we don't even care. That's real talk. We literally have just applied to two new lenders, and they both said, our credit looks great, and everything we sent them looks great. One of them said they'd be happy to do business with us. The other said, they didn't like us. They told us to move on. It's going to happen. It doesn't hurt our feelings. We ask what they're looking for. We'll figure it out and fix that issue. There are a lot of lenders out there, and they all view things a bit differently.

The more you do it, the more you'll learn from your experience. Seriously, don't be ashamed of being denied by a bank. Learn from that. That's the whole point. We don't get this type of education from our educational system or going to school. Nobody tells you in fifth grade, "Here's what you need to do to get a loan from a bank." It's so crucial to ask a loan officer what you need to do to be bankable.

Mike only has three loans in his name. That's why we want to emphasize so strongly to keep your W-2 job. Mike quit his job and wasn't able to get financed for a while. It really set him back. He had to prove himself as an entrepreneur, which takes two to three years. He had to wait a couple years before approaching the banks again for loans. Now that he was making money in this trade/profession, he had to ask if they'd lend him money again. They still weren't very comfortable with it. This is why we really stress leveraging that W-2 to get as many rental properties as you can. By going the traditional route, you can typically get a little bit cheaper interest rates with conventional mortgages in your personal name.

Get as many as you can. When you hit the threshold where they can't give you any more loans, then start looking at other banks for commercial loans. Get as many personal loans as you can for the lowest interest rate you can. Also, getting a personal loan allows you to amortize your loan over a longer period. Get the longest period you can, so you increase your cash flow.

We get two or three messages a week on different social media from people asking, "How do we get around the ten-property rule?" A lot of banks will only allow you to get up to ten loans in your personal name. Once you get above ten, they're not very willing to lend to you. They're in your personal name, and to them, it's high risk. At that point, they want you to have a business. We don't know all the rules, because the laws can change. However, we don't even have ten loans in our personal name. It's hard to get. They might not even necessarily be in your personal name, you could put them in an entity, but you'll be the guarantor.

Being Bankable

Go out and talk to Bankers. If they won't lend to you, just ask them what you need to do to become lendable. What is that going to take? They're going to tell you. They'll say something like, "Your credit score is a little low, or your debt-to-income ratio is a little high. Reduce some debt. Make a little more money if you can and pay off some bills or get that credit up." They'll essentially coach you on what you need to do to get a loan.

That's part of the reason it's very important to go and apply at a couple of banks. They will help you. They know what they need, and they'll figure out what you need to do far quicker than if you did the guesswork yourself. It may be hard news to hear if they can't lend you money. However, you have to bite that bullet and figure out what you need to do so they can lend you money. It's very important to apply to as many banks as you can, as quick as you can just to get the ball rolling. You need to find out what, if anything is adversely affecting your lendability or your ability to borrow money.

Know Your Numbers

We want to emphasize how important it is to know your numbers up front. We've talked about the "how-to's" of refinancing. But you really need to figure out what your monthly payment is going to be ahead of time. If you know your numbers, then work them backwards, to see if a new property is going to make sense to buy.

We use a spreadsheet. It gives us an estimated amortization schedule. We plug in what we plan on borrowing on a property, say $80,000. Then, if we amortize it over 20 years, we know what our monthly payment is going to be. Then we add in our insurance and taxes to figure out what our monthly cost will be. These numbers affect our cash flow. We need to know these numbers ahead of time. Checkout our website FreeLandlordCourse.com for more information.

The whole purpose of the BRRR strategy is to be able to acquire a lot of assets quickly with little to none of your own money. However, if you buy into a bad deal, it's not going to work out very well. The BRRRR strategy doesn't work well if the numbers don't make sense. What will happen is that when you refinance, the numbers are going to be less and less. The bank is going to give you less than what you might have borrowed to purchase and fix that property. Work these numbers backwards before you buy a property. Figure out what you think it might appraise for, and what you think you might get a loan for. Some lenders are going to lend different amounts and use different formulas in different areas. It's crucial to meet them and find out their lending criteria before you purchase a home. Know your numbers before you start. This will keep you from digging a hole you can't dig yourself out of. There's something to be said about a person who jumps in and takes action right away. Sometimes the best lessons are learned from mistakes. Don't be afraid to make mistakes either. However, there's a balance that needs to be struck. Take action, make mistakes, learn from them, but don't be reckless either.

Duration of The Loan

A loan terms to get familiar with is duration of the loan. When we get commercial loans, we're getting a three- or five-year term. That means it locks in the interest rate for that period of time. At the end of that term, the bank is going to do some due diligence to make sure we're paying our taxes, paying the bank, and that we're still lendable. They want to know if we're somebody they still want to do business with. Our commercial loans are typically one, three, or five years. We like to stretch these loans as far out as we can because we want to be locked into that interest rate. Rates are really low right now. They're historically low. If we can pay an extra quarter point of a historically low rate and get two more years guaranteed at that rate, that's what we'll do. Although we have our loans staggered. We have a mix of three- and five-year loans. We do that to limit risk.

Amortization

Amortization is very important. Term and amortization are very different but can often be confused for being the same thing. Amortization is the period over which the loan is financed. In other words, this is how long it would take to pay off the loan. Term is different, because that's how long the loan will be in place before the bank restructures the loan or requires you to get a new loan.

An amortization table is the pay scale in which the percentages of your payment go to interest versus principle. You absolutely want to become familiar with how that works, and how interest rates work. If you're new to this process or you want to get more involved in the BRRRR process, it's best to talk to a local banker, or several. Get to know these people, and get a relationship going with them. If they'll lend to you now, great, jump right in. If they won't lend to you now, that's okay too. Ask them what it would take to create a business relationship with them. They're going to look at your taxes, your W-2, and your debt to income ratio. They're going to look at your financials and be able to tell you what they'd need from you to do business with you. Most people don't realize this, but banks make their money by lending it. When someone deposits money into a bank, the bank is essentially losing money because they owe that person an interest rate on it. They actually use your money and lend it out to make themselves more money. Banks love lending money. However, they're protective about who they lend to. They don't want to lose money. Nobody wants to lose money. Banks get paid when they make loans.

Interest Rates

The next thing to get familiar with is interest rate. The interest rate is something you need to be aware of. There's a fixed interest rate loan versus an adjustable rate loan. Adjustable rate is very simple. It just means that the rate can adjust depending on the market. So shop around for different loans. Interest rates can vary quite a bit from bank to bank, as well as the other items we'll cover.

Some things to keep in mind about lending, the interest is paid very heavily upfront. In year one we're probably paying 90-

95% interest, and only 5-10% actually goes towards the principal balance of that loan. We make very little progress in the first few years towards paying down the principal balance of that house. That's why renewing a loan with the same bank, versus refinancing the loans with a different bank is such a powerful thing. We're also talking about two different types of loans too. We're talking about commercial loans. Commercial loans are what we're approved for, and super powerful. We're able to get more than those first traditional ten mortgages. A lot of people think they can only get approved for up to ten mortgages.

It is difficult to compare loans apples to apples because you cannot find out what rate you will get with each bank until you go through some underwriting. They can quote you the rate or a range of rates, but it will vary. Another option available to you is to pay points at closing. In essence, this is 'buying down' the interest rates. A point is equal to 1 percent of the mortgage. On a $100K mortgage a point is equal to $1,000. We don't buy down the rates but that is an option.

Loans can also be recourse or non-recourse loans. A recourse loan means you are personally liable for the debt even if it is lent to your entity. A non-recourse loan would only have the property as collateral for the debt and the lender could come after you for losses. Most lenders prefer recourse loans. In the beginning it is going to be very difficult if not impossible to get a non-recourse loan for your entity. You're probably going to have to vouch for your entity by being the personal guarantor on the loan. Makes sense since it is pretty easy to set up an LLC in most states.

When you are first starting out, you probably will not be able to negotiate much with the banks. You're going to be looking for anyone willing to lend. The more experienced you get and the more contacts you get in the banking sphere, the more you can determine what you want from a lender. It's rare you're going to be able to negotiate much on terms, but you can start to choose which banks you work with. The banks want to do business and loan money! Don't get a big head and start making unreasonable demands once you start working with a few banks. However, you can mention you'd prefer this or that, and see if your loan officer has the ability to work with you on rates or terms.

Traditional vs. Commercial Loans

There's a couple of differences between the traditional/conventional mortgages held in your personal name vs. commercial loans. With traditional loans, you're typically going to get fixed rates for 15-20-30 years, usually whatever the amortization is. You should be able to get the rate locked in for the length of the mortgage. That means the term and amortization table line up; they're both for 15, 20, 25 or even 30 years. We have a couple of 30-year loans in our personal names, where the term is 30 years. It's a fixed rate the entire time, because the amortization table is also for 30 years. However, commercial loans are different, and it can be a bit more confusing. They might be a variable rate. However, we always suggest getting a fixed rate mortgage, especially on low interest rate loans. Nobody wants their interest rate to go up. If the interest rate is already low, then with a variable rate loan the rate usually goes one way. It goes up. A fixed rate loan makes keeping track of everything easy too. With historically low rates, it just makes sense to lock in a low fixed rate than gamble with a variable rate.

Commercial Loans

With a commercial loan though, that's where things get a little different. The term and the amortization schedule don't usually line up. The amortization can be scheduled over a 20-year period usually. However, the term is going to be much shorter. This means that after a three- or five-year period, they're going to take another look at the loan. The lender wants to re-underwrite the loan essentially. They want to make sure you're still credit worthy, and paying them, the taxes, and the insurance on time. If the market interest rates have gone up, they'll want to increase the interest. They want to get paid what the market is offering.

With commercial loans, there's a little bit more variability and risk on you, the borrower. There's also a little bit more risk on the bank's part too, because they're loaning to an LLC, and not to you personally. Many of them will still make you sign a personal guarantee anyway. That's just a part of it. But it does affect their ability to collect in case of default.

We mentioned earlier that we like to work with small local banks that have around 3-5 branches. Let's discuss some benefits of working with these local banks. Local banks are more likely to invest in their community. When we're working with local banks, they can give us a loan on a property that is on a 20-year amortization schedule. However, the term might be three or five years. That's pretty standard. Most banks lean towards offering three-year loans. You might have to pay an extra quarter of a point or half a point to get the five-year term. When dealing with local banks, they're more likely to do portfolio lending, versus a bigger bank. This means they service the loans in house, rather than selling them off on the secondary market. This can be a huge advantage when that term comes due. At the end of that three year to five-year period, it might be hard to renew that loan if it was sold off to another bank, even though your loan is set for a 20-year amortization schedule.

If you don't have a bank that does portfolio lending, it's going to be very difficult to renew. That's a really big thing we want to harp on. Whenever the loans come due, they're just coming due for somebody to re-underwrite them at that bank. You're not having to go out and get another loan from a different bank necessarily. You can just get a new loan on it through the same bank. However, the bank usually does an appraisal, and they adjust the interest rate. Then they'll give you another three to five-year term. What's most important about this whole thing is that the amortization does not start back at day one. If we have a five-year term on a 20-year amortization schedule and we get through the first five years, then we'll be on year 6 of 20. However, if we refinance that loan with another bank at another 20-year amortization schedule, then we're starting at day one again. Earlier we said the first couple of years, 90-95% of our payment is going to the interest payments, not paying down the principal. Keeping the same amortization schedule is where the snowballing power really comes into play. Now we'll be paying down more of the principal than if we started over.

You want to keep your credit score and credit worthiness up since you will be re-underwritten every few years. The commercial lenders have asked for updated financials every year from us. It's best to keep a file of updated financials on hand ready to share with your new lending partners. We know people that complain about all the paperwork the banks require and bemoan the whole process. We look at it differently. To us, this is the real-life version of the Monopoly game. We are building wealth with someone else's money. If the banks want updated paperwork, we will come up with it. This is the game guys! Refinancing is the game. Another reason we love working with banks is it allows us to have very little skin in the game, and very little equity if we want. There is another more complex tool called equity stripping. That's when you actually refinance your portfolio and strip the equity out of them. This makes you less of a target for lawsuits, since you don't have assets with equity in them. 'Refi till you die' as Jason Hartman would say.

Recap:

1. **Getting Started:** Everyone has to start somewhere. We suggest keeping your W-2 job if you have one. Apply for loans at regional banks with 3-5 branches.

2. **Being Bankable:** When you apply for loans, banks will tell you if you qualify or not. If you get rejected, don't take it personally. Let them be your coach and figure out what you can improve. They might ask you to raise your credit score, lower your debt-to-income ratio, or pay off some debt.

3. **Know Your Numbers:** You have to know your numbers to leverage your money. If you don't know your numbers, or find good deals, you won't be able to pull all of your money out that you have invested. Eventually you'll get stuck or worse.

4. **Duration of The Loan:** This describes the length of the loan term before it gets rewritten by the underwriters.

5. **Amortization:** This is the schedule at which a loan is paid off. The interest is paid heavily up front compared to the principal.

6. **Interest Rates:** A fixed rate mortgage won't change the interest rate. However, an adjustable rate mortgage can change. With rates low right now, they'll most likely go up in the future. Lock in a fixed rate if you can. Adjustable rates are typical for commercial loans.

7. **Personal Loans Vs. Commercial Loans:** Personal loans are generally 15-20-30-year term loans. Commercial loans usually have to be re-underwritten every 3-5 years.

Action Item: Talk to bankers!! We've mentioned this throughout the book, but it bears repeating. The sooner you start applying for loans, the better equipped you'll be to refinance when the time comes. We suggest focusing on small regional banks with 3-5 branches to take advantage of portfolio lending.

"If you don't understand leverage, you're working too hard."

-Anonymous

PART VI

REPEAT

CHAPTER 20

Repeat

We want to keep this strategy simple, and it is simple. This one thing we have said in previous chapters as well as in our previous book, 'The Ultimate Guide to Wholesaling Real Estate', Keep it simple. The BRRRR strategy is simple, it's just Buy, Rehab, Rent, Refinance, and Repeat. We've made it to Repeat. This is where the strategy becomes so powerful. If you refinance most or all of your money out, you get to use it all over again and again to acquire more cash flowing rentals. This is the magic of BRRRR. The ability to do this one time or 20 or even 100 times is what makes it so powerful.

If you are working full time and you just did this twice a year as your part time job, in 10 years you could have 20 rental properties. If your metrics are similar to ours and your cash flow is just $300 per property per month that is $6,000 per month in extra income, or $72,000 annually. That replaces most people's full-time income. The average income in the U.S. is around $59,037 (according to the BLS for 2017). In 10 years, you created an income stream of $72,000 per year! REPEAT is where the real power of this strategy comes into play. You do not need a TON of money to do this. You only need to find enough money to fund one rental property at a time. You'll also get better each time you purchase another property because you will have learned from experience. If you want financial freedom, there is no reason you cannot replace a full-time income in 10 years or less.

However, we realize that the real world is not that straight forward as we laid out in this book. Whether you are working on your 4th or 14th project, and you're trying to work your full-time job, you'll also want to spend time with the family and relax. This can be difficult while managing a rental rehab on top of getting a call from another tenant about a leaky sink. It can be overwhelming. So what do you do? You have to develop systems and start getting others to help you. In the "Rent" section of the book, we talked about getting a property manager when you get around 10 doors. Adjust that as needed. Use this model as you see fit. If you're working full time and you can't handle the property management, you might have to factor that cost into your cash flow number. It is very important to put systems in place to help you REPEAT.

In order to REPEAT and REPEAT and REPEAT, we believe it is important for you to know your reason for 'why' you are doing this. Not everyone's reasons will be the same. We recommend Simon Sinek's book "Start with Why". At minimum, you could use the exercise from his book. Ask yourself, "Why do I want to do this?" Then take that answer and ask "why?" again. Take that answer and ask "why?" again. You need to do this until you can't really drill down any deeper. This is your real motivation; this is your true reason why. Thinking about this should drive you to get up early and work on BRRRR or start grinding away after you just worked all day.

Once you have a good idea of your real motivations, we like to paint a vision of where we are going and how we are going to get there by using a GOSPA plan. GOSPA is an acronym for

Goals, Objectives, Strategy, Plans, Activities. You start with the big picture goals you want to achieve, then you drill down all the way to the activities that need to be done.

We have some great tips in our first book, "The Ultimate Guide to Wholesaling." In that book, we discuss the importance of building a dream team, how to be a leader, how to get the right mindset when things get tough, how to be a "rhino" to just get things done. We also talk about business planning, starting the day off right, the value of a mentor or coach, different exit strategies, and the importance of furthering education. Below is just a refresher for those who've read that book. And if you haven't read that book, hopefully this will serve as a primer to illustrate the importance of these concepts.

Dream Team

You can't do everything on your own. It's not practical from a time perspective, not to mention, you should hire professionals to do the work you're not qualified to do.

- Pitfalls of a solopreneur- Sharing in success makes things easier. We would all love to have a smaller piece of a bigger pie than go at it alone.

- Real Estate Agents- These people can be great for getting leads.

- CPA's- Getting a qualified CPA to help you develop a tax strategy will save you a lot of money in the long run.

- Virtual Assistants- We couldn't scale the way we have without them as a part of our team. They are Rockstar's.

- Junior Buyers- They often bring us deals, or they find buyers for deals we're having trouble selling. We get so many leads now that we can't handle them all. Our junior buyers help with that too.

- Students- One of the best ways to learn is to teach. It feels great too.

Be A Rhino

Having the right mindset might be your biggest obstacle. We all have fears, it's how you manage them that will make or break your success. You've just gotta make things happen. Also, when you get the ball rolling, you can't let up. Strike while the iron is hot. It's important to handle setbacks appropriately, because they're inevitable. That's part of the learning process though. Keep evolving. Don't forget, an entrepreneur is a person who solves problems for profit or pay. You're in this business because you're a problem solver, never forget that. Solving problems is how you create value.

Yes, there are always going to be fears that creep into your mind. That's part of human nature, the fear of "what if." What if the tenants all don't pay? What if one of the houses burns down? What if we can't get this property refinanced? What if we have one or two million dollars in debt and can't pay it back? There are always fears and reasons not to do something. You have to have a strong enough reason why, to help you blow through these obstacles. These are all excuses. If the tenants don't pay, you'll have to evict them and find a new tenant that will. You have insurance on your properties if they burn down. If you can't get a property to refinance for the number you need you can go to another bank, or you can sell it if you just rehabbed it. The middle class is afraid; the upper class uses that to their advantage and leverages money.

Start the Day Right

We're big fans of Hal Elrod, and his book "Miracle Morning." Starting your day right is crucial to your success. You need to start with high energy. Break out of mediocrity. He uses a method called SAVERS

- Silence- Meditation or prayer

- Affirmations- Reminding yourself you're worthy, powerful, confident, etc. Affirmations rewire your brain for success.

- Visualization- Making what you want visual makes it seem so much more real in our minds.

- Exercise- It's so important to be healthy to maintain the energy levels needed to be successful

- Reading- Ongoing education is motivating and has such real-world applications. It can save or make you thousands or 10's of thousands over the course of a year.

- Scribing- Journaling is such a powerful way to understand where your mind is at. It's a great way to handle overwhelm.

Other Exit Strategies

As you progress in your real estate career, you'll find more opportunities that you didn't see before. You'll find niches that might suit your investing needs better. Here is a brief overview of other real estate exit strategies.

- Retail Rehab- This is when you rehab a property for sale on the retail market, rather than holding onto it as a rental. These are high risk, high reward projects. However, when done right, they are a very lucrative way to make money in real estate.

- Subject To- This is when you buy a property "subject-to" the existing mortgage. These are great, because you don't have to get a loan in your name if that's an issue.

- Owner Financing- This is when you buy a property from the current owner without going to a bank for financing. The owner holds the note, and acts as the bank.

- Lease Option- This allows you to lease a property without having to buy it. Instead, you get the "option" to buy it later at a predetermined price. This is another effective way to take control of a property without getting a loan in your name.

If you are not going directly to sellers for leads you need a good wholesaler and real estate agent to bring you leads. Both on and off market leads.

We have a lot going on at the discount property investors; we wholesale we buy and manage rentals we podcast, and we help coach others to do the same. We are busy and figuring out what to do when is a challenge. Each year and then quarterly we go through the GOSPA Plan and Traction Plan (check out the book Traction by Gino Wickman) to determine what our goals are going to be for the next year and each quarter. So, we divided up who is in charge of what and then they get it done that quarter. It's like that old anecdote: "How do you eat an elephant? One bite at a time."

Furthering Education

Below are some of the books we recommend you read. They have helped transform our wholesaling business.

- *"12 Week Year"* by Brian P. Moran
- *"Rich Dad, Poor" Dad* by Robert Kiyosaki
- *"Start With Why"* by Simon Sinek
- *"The 10x Rule"* by Grant Cardone
- *"The Four-Hour Work Week"* by Tim Ferriss
- *"The Miracle Morning"* by Hal Elrod
- *"Traction"* by Gino Wickman
- *"The Rhythm of Life"* by Matthew Kelly
- "The 7 Habits of Highly Effective People" by Stephen Covey
- "The Power of Habit" by Charles Duhigg
- "Go for No" by Richard Fenton & Andrea Waltz
- "The One Thing" by Gary Keller

Our Personal Plan

What do we plan to do with our rentals? We think as real estate investors, we should always think long-term. As a team, we plan to get 150 houses. That's 50 houses per person. That is just the beginning for us. We will probably get there by the time this book is published. The idea was that it's an easy number divided between the three owners. We could disperse them, or we might sell them off and start over, or refinance them into larger apartment buildings. Having control over assets gives you power and freedom. Once you have 50 rentals, the cash flow gives you options. You don't need to keep working that day job if you don't want to. The tax laws are written to your advantage. We can hold them for 27 and a half years and then 1031 exchange them into another property, deferring the taxes even further.

1031 Exchanges

You can save yourself from paying a lot of taxes via depreciation. Then when you've hit your maximum allotted depreciation per property (27.5 years) you can sell that property in "exchange" for a new one and avoid getting taxed on that income. That's why it's called a 1031 exchange. 1031 just refers to a section in the tax code.

A 1031 exchange is a way to defer your recognition of that capital gain. If you buy a property, you'll be saving on taxes by using depreciation. However, you'll have to pay back those tax savings when you sell that property that you depreciated. However, if you invest that income into another property, you're able to defer that gain. A 1031 exchange allows you to not pay taxes on a gain because you're reinvesting it.

The way a 1031 exchange works, is a third party, like a title company, a lawyer, or a 1031 exchange company holds your money after you sell a property. Then you can go buy another asset with it, and do not have to pay back those tax benefits you received through depreciation. It's a way to defer those taxes.

There are even tax benefits that you're able to transfer to your heirs. It doesn't matter if you own the home in a trust, or an LLC. This is a bit complicated, and builds on the depreciation you took before, and has to do with inheritance. It is a BIG deal though and has to do with building and transferring generational wealth in your family. Anytime you own a piece of real estate and you die; you can pass that real estate on to your heirs. Even if you took depreciation over 27.5 years. The way it works with the current laws of inheritance, is that when a property passes to a new person, the basis resets. This is HUGE. This is in reference to the depreciation we just mentioned. Whatever the current value of the property is, that's the value the property starts at. The heirs have the ability to start depreciating the property again on their taxes. Or if they sell it, they would only pay income taxes on the new basis value vs the sale price, rather than a property depreciated to zero. You only pay taxes when there is a gain.

Depreciation is a huge tax advantage of owning rental properties. When the property is depreciated to zero, there is no longer that tax advantage. This is one way to avoid paying the taxes on the appreciated value of the asset based on the depreciated value. Don't forget, we believe that taxes were invented as a way to protect the wealthy. We're not suggesting that's right or wrong. However, since we can't change the tax code, we decided to learn how it works so we can use it to our advantage. Those are some of the tax benefits of owning real estate or rental properties essentially. You can also go through something called the "board of appeals" to appeal the assessed value of a property and try to get a lower tax rate. We are not suggesting that anyone avoid paying taxes or do anything illegal. We're just saying that there are legal ways to lower your taxes. This is huge because taxes are one of every business biggest expense.

Final Thoughts

We suggest you learn real estate primarily via wholesaling. Once you find a good deal you have options; you can rehab it, you can keep it as a rental, or you can wholesale it. You can do a lot of things. It all starts with finding the deal. As of today, we own around 100 doors (rental properties) between our individual and company portfolios. Mike is more involved with the rental side of the business. It's one of his favorite things. He's really good at it and does it day in and day out. Dave does a lot more on the wholesale side of the business. We divide and conquer. By creating a team, we can do more together. If we were trying to do this on our own, we could do it, but it would be slow and inefficient. By working together and building a team dynamic we've maximized our output. If you don't have a partner or a team already, it's definitely something you should consider. Even if it is just one other person, you'll get more done. Teams get things done.

We wholesale and buy rentals. We try to keep what works best for us and sell the rest. Just because a property doesn't fit our criteria, doesn't mean it's not a perfect fit for one of our buyers. We encourage you to do the same. Wholesaling is a job, and it does require a lot of work. However, you can put that work to use by buying rental properties so you can actually make money while you sleep. We have helped literally thousands of people learn to wholesale online at <u>FreeWholesaleCourse.com</u> and in our first book *"The Ultimate Guide to Wholesaling Real Estate"*. We consider wholesaling a steppingstone into buying rentals or other forms of real estate investing. It's especially useful if you're starting with little cash and little knowledge. For more information about rental property, examples of leases, spreadsheets we use, and videos of property walkthroughs, visit our site <u>FreeLandlordCourse.com.</u>

Recap:

1. **Repeat:** Repeating is crucial to the BRRRR method. This is where the magic happens, and the ball really gets rolling. Make sure you systemize your process, so you can get help from others.

2. **Dream Team:** You can't do this alone, nor should you. Hire professionals for work you're not qualified to do. To scale this business, you have to delegate work to others.

3. **Be A Rhino:** Mindset is everything in the game of real estate. Stop at nothing, and nothing can stop you.

4. **Start The Day Right:** Go into each day prepared, with high energy, and a clear mind.

5. **Other Exit Strategies:** With experience, you'll find more creative ways to make money. There are a lot of niches that might interest you.

6. **Furthering Education:** The books we've read have transformed our business. We couldn't do what we've done without constantly learning.

7. **Our Personal Plan:** We plan on owning 150 rental properties within our business, then we'll go our separate ways. It's very important to start with the end in mind, especially with business partners. We have a lofty goal, but we're getting close to achieving it.

8. **1031 Exchanges:** Taxes are one of our biggest expenses. However, we can defer taxes legally using 1031 exchanges. This is a great way to build generational wealth.

9. **Final Thoughts:** Success doesn't happen overnight, but it will happen if you keep working at it. We believe everyone should start their real estate career wholesaling. It's low risk, fast cash, and is a great way to learn your numbers while finding great deals. The BRRRR model is dependent on finding great deals.

Action Item: Go back through the book, and glance at the action items. Did you complete them, or just skim over them. Reading is a great way to learn. However, at the end of the day, the only real learning occurs via taking action. Every step is important to your success.

"Many will start fast. Few will finish strong." -Gary Ryan Blair

Epilogue

A sincere thank you to our friend and editor Eric Cain. Eric helped us compile this book and is as integral a part of it coming to life as either of us. Thank you!

Erik Cain (ghostwriter/editor) has done it all. He's a self-proclaimed "Jack of all trades, master of fun." He's gone from lifeguard to lumberjack, from camp counselor to park ranger, and from firefighter to Rockstar, and real estate tycoon (Ok. The last two might be a bit of a stretch, but he's a legend in his own mind).

Erik's entrepreneurial bug bit him when a friend gave him the book, "The 4-Hour Work Week" by Tim Ferriss. He realized his life goal was to never be bored. He started his real estate career flipping houses and wholesaling deals, all while building a modest rental portfolio to establish a stream of passive income.

After 5 years of real estate, he got bored yet again, and wanted to try something new (pick a lane Erik). Through years of job hopping, he came to understand that his true passion and favorite creative outlet was teaching and writing. He reached out to an old soccer teammate from high school (David Dodge). He knew that David worked with Virtual Assistants (VA's). And thus, asked David if he'd be willing to leave Erik a reference on Upwork.com. David, true to his integrity and win-win mentality, asked, "Before I do that, can you actually edit?" Then he offered Erik a job. Utilizing his own real estate knowledge and passion for teaching, Erik helped Mike and David use their own podcasts to put together the book you're reading now.

While editing the Discount Property Investors podcast transcripts, Erik revived his interest in Real Estate. Instead of selling his properties, he systemized his rental business to run without him. His rental income now pays for his travels. He can often be found traveling to exotic parts of the world living the "Four Hour Work Week" lifestyle.

If you are interested in writing your own book, or need editing, you can contact Erik at Erik.b.cain@gmail.com

Made in the USA
Monee, IL
15 April 2022

94797230R00213